D0891466

THE REGULATED INDUSTRIES
AND THE ECONOMY

Also by Paul W. MacAvoy

THE CRISIS OF THE REGULATORY COMMISSIONS

ECONOMIC PERSPECTIVE ON THE POLITICS OF
INTERNATIONAL COMMODITY AGREEMENTS

THE ECONOMICS OF THE NATURAL GAS SHORTAGE

The
Regulated Industries
and the Economy

Paul W. MacAvoy

This is a special edition prepared for
The Presidents Association

W · W · NORTON & COMPANY
NEW YORK   LONDON

Library of Congress Cataloging in Publication Data
MacAvoy, Paul W
  The regulated industries and the economy.

  Includes index.
  1. Industry and state—United States.
2. Trade regulation—United States. I. Title.
HD3616.U47M23 1979   338.973   79-15457
ISBN 0-393-01280-8
ISBN 0-393-95094-8 pbk.

1 2 3 4 5 6 7 8 9 0

For Katherine

Contents

⟨⟨◇◇◇⟩⟩

CONTENTS

Preface

◇◇◇◇◇

In its first fifty years, regulation seemed to be the solution to the problem of excessively powerful control by business of retail markets. But even while this solution was being tried, the regulatory agencies were given further tasks. In particular, the regulatory commissions were to compel suppliers to fulfill expanded obligations to provide adequate service, even in unprofitable markets. Commissions were to foster industry development, reduce discrimination, and stabilize prices over the business cycle as well. Because of these diverse motives, regulation continued to expand both in the number of industries covered and in the ways in which these industries were controlled.

This expansion was gradual at first but, since the late 1960s, the growth of agency control has been explosive. The motive then was to use the regulatory process to increase health, safety, and the quality of the environment. By the 1970s, regulation had become so extensive that it had begun to have measurable effects on the overall economic condition of the country as well as on the provision of goods and services in certain markets. As a result, general public interest in the impact of all of this regulation has grown.

Various and numerous studies have attempted to evaluate the effects of the control process on the regulated industries. This book compiles, updates, and extends these studies to include assessments of the old price controls under the new inflationary conditions, and of the new health and environmental controls. In so doing, it provides a critique of regulation's results as of the late 1970s. This examination reveals that regulation has reduced the quality and even the quantity of output in the most affected industries. The economy as a whole has been impacted in the same way, as regulation has grown. These results cause some concern for the condition and for the expansion of the economy in the 1980s.

Reform of regulation and, specifically, deregulation could very well improve on this performance. But reform and deregulation are institutionalized political processes not that different from regulation. Steps to achieve them can have adverse effects of their own on the various industries and on the economy. Moreover, problems arise when the interest groups now helped (or hindered) by regulation do not share equally in the benefits from change. Thus, significant change in the way in which regulation operates is not very likely.

Our projection, based on the political and economic behavior observed in this decade, is that the regulated industries will continue into the 1980s operating on the basis of rules and procedures established by the agencies in the last set of cases. This will have a deleterious impact on the future growth of the regulated industries and thus on the size of the economy. But it is hoped that this volume will help clarify the problems from continuing regulation as usual, and thus that this bleak outlook can be modified.

These findings and predictions are products of the research program on government-business relations at the Yale School of Organization and Management. Funded by the General Electric Foundation, the Carthage Foundation, the J. M. Foundation, the Walker Foundation, the Gulf Foundation, the Pfizer Educational Fund, and IBM Corporation, the program attempts to measure and evaluate change on the boundary between private- and public-sector activities. The support provided by this program is gratefully acknowledged, for otherwise detailed investigations of each of the industries and agencies could not have been undertaken. At Yale, the development of analytical files on particular regulated industries was the task of my able research assistants, James Baker, Andrew Carron, Steven Felgran, Eric Mankin, David Mirchin, Laura Scher, Curtis Spraitzer, Craig Stewart, Gail Trask, and Robert Yedid. Their zealous efforts to find data and studies are much appreciated. Then, too, my readers have added much by deleting errors and pointing out omissions; they include Frank Borman, Gordon Corey, Harland Dellsey, George Haefelein, Geoffrey Hazard, Paul Joskow, James C. Miller, III, Jonathan Rose, Stephen Ross, Kenneth Robinson, and John Snow. I am most grateful for their assistance but cannot ask them to share responsibility for the results.

April 1979

THE REGULATED INDUSTRIES
AND THE ECONOMY

1

◇━◇━◇━◇━◇

The Spread of Regulation
and the Birth of Deregulation

ALTHOUGH GOVERNMENT control of American industry and trade dates from colonial times, specific and detailed price and entry regulation began only ninety years ago. Passage of the Act to Regulate Commerce (1887), which established federal jurisdiction over interstate railroad rates and service, marked this beginning. Since then, and particularly since the 1930s, regulatory agencies have set prices and certified the services of utilities and of companies providing transportation of passengers and freight. Within the last two decades, regulatory controls have been extended to cover, directly, natural gas and petroleum products companies and, indirectly, health services organizations. Regulation has spread even further as state and federal agencies have been set up in the past few years to control environmental quality and workplace health and safety conditions throughout all of industry and trade.

As regulation has expanded, so has the movement for deregulation. It is to be expected that increased regulatory activity would provoke more efforts to reform particular agencies, both in the state capitols and in Washington. However, recent proposals for reform have gone beyond simply making corrections in an agency procedure. For example, the Ford administration went so far as to propose legislation seeking to eliminate federal price-setting authority over airlines, trucking companies, banking institutions, and gas producers. While these initiatives did not become laws, Congress did pass legislation eliminating the federal apparatus underlying fair-trade retail prices and removing some controls over railroad rates and stock brokerage fees. During the Carter administration bills were passed calling for "phased" airline rate deregulation and natural gas deregulation by the early 1980s.[1] Both administrations made extensive efforts to reorganize agency activities or change agency decisions in order to reduce the operation of existing regulation.

Although improvements in the operation of the regulatory commissions had been made previously, the Ford and Carter reform initiatives were more comprehensive and radical. For the first time, they restricted regulation itself, rather than simply adjusting or extending agency prerogatives. Legislative as well as organizational change sought to remove controls and to establish limits on further expansion of agency authority.

Proponents of this new approach have also argued that regulation of health, safety, and environmental quality did not offer much hope for good results. They pointed out that the rapid and widespread extension of the new health and safety regulations increased overall costs by requiring new operations under complicated, highly detailed, and at times arbitrary control programs. President Ford based his call for across-the-board reform in 1975 on a study which estimated that regulatory costs to the economy were more than $100 billion per year.[2] Although costs of control were not this great, as has been implied by later, more detailed assessments, what was evident nevertheless was that the costs from regulatory activity had increased and that they had begun to have an impact on how the economy operated. In addition, the benefits sought from regulation were not as evident as its costs and they seem to have fallen far short of statutory goals to create a safe and clean economy.[3]

Although attempts were made in the late 1970s to deregulate

specific industries, there was substantial overall regulatory growth. Even so, the case for deregulation can still be made across these industries. This case gathers evidence as the specific effects of controls on quantity, quality, and growth of services become more known in the regulated industries. If service is adversely affected and significantly so, then the system is not working. Thus general and specific deregulation is in order.

The first step in evaluating whether regulation in fact does have such effects is to determine the impact on prices and services both from price regulation in the transportation and public utilities and from the safety, health, and environmental regulations imposed on all industries. Such an assessment is made here with respect to how well the regulated sectors of the economy have functioned under the economic and social conditions that have characterized the last decade. Indeed, the findings are that these industries have done less well than others, in ways attributable to regulation. As a result, the final chapter takes up the question of whether further reforms including deregulation can improve industry and economy performance.

The Characteristics and Growth of Regulation

Traditionally controls have centered on regulating prices and entry of companies in interstate transportation (both railroads and trucking firms), communications (telephones and broadcasting), electricity production, and pipeline transportation. The federal agencies performing these functions are indicated in Table 1.1. In most of these industries, price levels have been controlled by commission or agency review in courtlike proceedings on company requests for increases. At both the state and federal levels of government, commissions have also determined price differences for varying types of service and have set entry conditions into most or all markets providing these services. They have moni-

TABLE 1.1 *Industries Subject to Price and Entry Regulation*

Industry	Jurisdiction and extent of regulation
Electricity generation	Federal Energy Regulatory Commission and 49 state agencies control prices; 35 state agencies certify service.
Natural-gas transmission and retail distribution	Federal Energy Regulatory Commission controls interstate transportation and 49 state agencies set rates for distribution.
Telephone services	Federal Communications Commission and 50 state agencies set rates, entry, and service conditions.
Airline services	Civil Aeronautics Board regulations set fares and entry conditions before the Airline Deregulation Act of 1978; 21 state agencies set fare and entry conditions interstate.
Highway freight services	Interstate Commerce Commission and 47 state agencies regulate rates; the ICC and 45 state agencies control entry into common-carrier services.
Railroad transportation	Interstate Commerce Commission and 44 state agencies set freight rates; the ICC and 26 state agencies certify entry into the provision of rail services.

SOURCE: *The Challenge of Regulatory Reform: A Report to the President from the Domestic Council Review Group on Regulatory Reform* (Washington, D.C.: U.S. Government Printing Office, 1977), pp. 50–51; *1976 Annual Report on Utility and Carrier Regulation* (Washington, D.C.: National Association of Regulatory Utility Commissioners, 1977), pp. 392, 488, 594, 612, 615. See also Appendix Tables A.1 and A.2.

tored service quality and extended service coverage to include new communities, customers and conveniences.

These commissions and agencies were established for different reasons in different industries. For instance, they gained jurisdiction over railroads in response to public antagonism toward oligopolistic pricing practices. Concern that single-supplier market conditions in the gas, electric, and telephone industries would leave consumers open to monopoly pricing determined the jurisdiction imposed over these sectors. Controls were intended to keep consumer prices at the unit costs of providing service—approximating competitive pricing—rather than allowing the producers to use their single-supplier powers to set prices above unit costs so as to generate excessive profits.

Even at the beginning, however, these agencies were also justified on grounds that controls were needed to improve the quality or increase the volume of service in these particular industries. The history of regulatory legislation contains many complaints about discriminatory, limited, or poor quality service; and numerous recommendations were made for ways that regulation could stimulate more local service. To provide more service, however, often required extending existing systems so that some unregulated prices were below costs. To achieve this extension, and keep such a firm in business, regulation itself had to allow the company to charge higher-than-competitive prices on some other services.

The justifications used to initiate controls have also been invoked to extend regulation. The lower-consumer-prices rationale is behind the extension of energy regulation to natural-gas field prices in the 1950s and to crude-oil and refined petroleum products after the OPEC oil embargo of 1973. Service-quality regulation was extended to the trucking and airline industries as these industries developed and spread across the country in the 1930s. While the Motor Carrier Act of 1935 sought to "promote adequate, economical, and efficient service by motor carriers," it also set as a goal that regulation "develop and preserve a highway transportation system adapted to the needs of the commerce of the United States."[4] The House Report accompanying the Civil Aeronautics Act of 1938 set out as the purpose of regulation not only to prevent unduly high air fares, but also to prevent "competing carriers from engaging in rate wars which would be disasterous to all concerned" and to bring an end to "this chaotic situation of the air carriers [which] has shake[n] the faith of the investing public in the financial stability and prevent[ed] the flow of funds into this industry."[5] These rationales also entered into federal regulation of telephone services, where both reduction of prices and extension of consumer services were to be pursued by the Federal Communications Commission. An expression of such purposes is found in the Communications Act of 1934: ". . . to make available so far as possible to all people of the United States a rapid, efficient, nationwide, and worldwide wire and cable service with adequate facilities at reasonable charges."[6]

Regulation was not limited to such price-control and service-enhancement policies. It was part of a number of early attempts to improve health, safety, and working conditions as well. Particularly important initiatives were the Food and Drug Administration, set up in 1931, and the Federal Aviation Administration, set up in 1948. They served as models for setting standards to improve product or service safety. However, the majority of federal agencies that are responsible for setting performance standards were established in the last ten years (see Table 1.2). The most significant of these are the Environmental Protection Agency (EPA) and the Occupational Safety and Health Administration (OSHA). Both have had an impact on production conditions in almost every industry. The agency having the most comprehensive authority in a single industry is the National Highway Traffic Safety Administration (NHTSA), which sets performance standards for automobiles.

These regulatory organizations have mostly been justified on grounds that private producers fail to take account of the full social costs of their activities and, where this results in unhealthy conditions, controls should require the companies to provide more health or safety. The rationales of particular agencies imply different kinds of regulation, but the general basis of operations for all these new agencies is to prevent harm from a process, product, or their side effects.[7]

How extensive is the coverage of the economy by regulation? The regulatory agencies engage in a broad range of control activities, now accounting for federal administrative expenditures of slightly more than $3 billion per year.[8] This figure alone is not indicative of regulation's full impact on economic activity. Indeed, if regulatory activity were concentrated in a single industry, or even in a few industries, it would not have any widespread economic impact. But, in fact, a few dollars of regulatory activity initiate controls over a substantial and increasing share of private-sector industry and trade.

The coverage of controls is indicated by accumulating industry by industry the share of national output produced under regulation (as in Table 1.3). The national product of the public utilities and the transportation companies under the jurisdiction of price-regulating commissions accounts for somewhat more than 5 percent of total gross national product (GNP). When this regulatory process was extended to petroleum production, refining, and marketing in the mid-1970s, another 3 percent of GNP was brought under agency surveillance. The financial sector, accounting for approximately 3 percent of GNP, typically has had controls on entry, service offerings, and interest rates, at either the national or state level.

By far the most significant growth of regulation, in terms of coverage of the economy, occurred with the establishment of agencies to increase workers' health and safety (OSHA) and to protect the environment (EPA). Their controls cover virtually every manufacturer regardless of industry. In practice, however, only a few industries were seriously enough affected to adjust pricing, production, and investment decisions; the other industries were not significantly affected because their particular production

TABLE 1.2 *Regulating Health, Safety, and the Quality of the Environment*

Organization	Regulatory function	Year established
The Packers and Stockyards Administration, Department of Agriculture	Determines plant conditions and business practices in livestock and processed-meat production so as to provide healthful meat products.	1916
The Food and Drug Administration, Department of Health, Education and Welfare	Controls the labeling and content of foods and drugs.	1931
The Agricultural Marketing Service, Department of Agriculture	Determines healthful standards for most farm commodities and also sets minimum prices for milk in some areas.	1937
The Federal Aviation Administration, Department of Transportation	Operates air-traffic-control systems and sets safety standards for aircraft and airports to reduce accidents.	1948
The Animal and Plant Health Inspection Service, Department of Agriculture	Sets standards for plant safety and inspects and enforces laws relating to meat and poultry quality.	1953
The Federal Highway Administration, Department of Transportation	Sets safety regulations for interstate trucking services.	1966
The Federal Railroad Administration, Department of Transportation	Sets safety standards for interstate railroad transportation.	1970

TABLE 1.2 (Continued)

Agency	Function	Year
The National Highway Traffic Safety Administration, Department of Transportation	Sets safety standards for automobiles so as to reduce highway accident fatalities.	1970
The Environmental Protection Agency	Develops environmental quality standards and approves abatement plans operated by state agencies to curtail individual industry pollution emissions.	1970
The Consumer Product Safety Commission	Sets product safety standards.	1972
The Mining Enforcement and Safety Administration, Department of the Interior	Sets mine safety standards.	1973
The Drug Enforcement Administration, Department of Justice	Controls trade in narcotics and drugs.	1973
The Occupational Safety and Health Administration, Department of Labor	Sets and enforces workers' safety and health regulations to reduce work-related accident and disease.	1973
The Nuclear Regulatory Commission	Licenses the construction and operation of civilian nuclear power plants and other uses of nuclear energy.	1975

SOURCE: *The Challenge of Regulatory Reform: A Report to the President from the Domestic Council Review Group on Regulatory Reform* (Washington, D.C.: U.S. Government Printing Office, 1977), pp. 50–54.

processes allowed either virtually costless adoption of the rules or, more likely, because standards and enforcement had not been worked out for them.

The mining, construction, and chemical industries were regulated in the sense that large parts of their investments had been diverted to meet regulatory equipment requirements. The paper, primary metal, motor vehicle, stone, clay and glass product, and petroleum refining industries were not required to make such investments in plant and equipment, but they were regulated because of controls on key production processes or products from specific work-safety rules and pollution-emission restrictions. These industries together produce almost 12 percent of GNP. Thus the regulated sector of the economy comprises nearly 24 percent of GNP (as shown in Table 1.3). This percentage is large enough to at least raise questions about the regulated economy and the possibility that controls have been extended to cover too much and too many private sector activities. Before dealing with such questions, however, one must reflect on how these agencies operate.

The Regulatory Process

What do these regulatory agencies actually do and how do they do it? Each regulatory agency begins with a different function, but a uniformity of process can be observed which allows generalizations about performance. Each agency has political appointees as executives to make decisions, a permanent staff to administer the decisions, and substantial financial support to carry out operations. Decisions and operations are to carry out the mandate in the statute provided by the legislature. As the agency develops, these procedures and decisions, if not goals, tend to resemble other agencies. A set of rather narrow practices becomes controlling with respect to case decisions. Thus the regulatory organization's behavior may well be predictable within a range.

TABLE 1.3 *Percent of GNP in the Regulated Sector of the Economy* [a]

Category	Percent of GNP under regulation in 1965	Percent of GNP under regulation in 1975
Price regulation [b]	5.5	8.8
Financial markets regulation [c]	2.7	3.0
Health and safety regulation [d]	—	11.9
Total	8.2	23.7

[a] The calculations are industry-group gross products originating as a percentage of all-industry gross product originating. Industries are defined as including those companies or activities accounted for in the Department of Commerce Standard Industrial Classification (with SIC codes shown after each industry).

[b] Includes Railroads (40), Motor Freight Transportation and Warehousing (42), Air Transportation (45), Communications (48), Electric, Gas, and Sanitary Services (49), and Crude Petroleum and Natural Gas (13) for 1975 only (SIC codes in parentheses).

[c] Includes Banking (60) and Insurance (63).

[d] Includes Metal Mining (10), Coal Mining (11–12), Mining and Quarrying of Nonmetallic Minerals (14), Construction (15–17), Paper and Allied Products (26), Chemical and Allied Products (28), Petroleum and Related Industries (29), Stone, Clay, and Glass Products (32), Primary Metal Industries (33), Motor Vehicles and Equipment (371).

SOURCE: U.S. Department of Commerce, *Workfile 1205-02-02*. 1976 revision.

Regardless of the industry being regulated, the various agencies, boards, and commissions use many of the same arguments and factual indicators of conditions. Although they respond to the requests of the companies for changes by taking a wide range of testimony and evidence, in practice certain physical and financial accounting measures of previous activities are used as the basis for their decisions. This accounting approach to evidence is constraining in ways that maintain decisions and thus establish the behavior of the regulated companies. In price-regulation cases, revenue increases are justified by changes in historical costs as shown in financial reports. In health or safety regulations, controls are placed on equipment specified by engineering studies. This results in present and near-future behavior set in line with past performance, and thus in marked stability when compared with change in the unregulated industries.

There are a number of factors, but principally two, that make for such operating uniformity. First, the legislative mandates of different agencies have been similar, in some cases going so far as to couch their purposes in the same language. For instance, the goals in the Act to Regulate Commerce of 1887—stabilizing prices, expanding service, and promoting equity in railroad fare structures—were repeated in later transportation regulatory statutes. Both state and national statutes establishing agencies to control the prices of electricity, gas, and telephone services repeated admonitions against discriminatory, unstable, and high prices, and most also set out requirements for more and better service in these industries. To be sure, the commissions controlling health, safety, and environmental conditions were called upon to solve different problems, but even then similarities of language in limiting controls to what was practicable in the market implied application of roughly the same process as for calculating costs in price regulation.

The second factor has been the Administrative Procedures Act and its recourse to court review.[9] This general law sets requirements for open hearings, presentation of evidence, and case-decision justification in most of the agencies. By allowing the courts to review the agency's decisions for openness of process and due consideration of the evidence presented, the act naturally leads agencies to emphasize quantitative rather than judgmental or predictive materials. The courtlike proceedings under the act emphasize evidence on existing conditions, thereby taking less account of future or present opportunity losses from alternatives not in operation. The expanding scope of judicial review has encompassed issues not only as to whether a statute is being complied with, but also whether the procedures chosen by the agencies are "reasonable," and whether, indeed, the results themselves are "reasonable."[10] The determination to avoid unfavorable review on these new issues has required the agencies to establish even more case procedural conformity.

This case process has itself set limits on price increases in the public-utility and transportation industries. The agencies evaluate requests for price or rate increases by holding them to the sum of recent period operating costs, depreciation, and taxes along with a "reasonable profit." The profit estimates mostly are arrived at by multiplying a determined "reasonable" rate of return times the capital rate base, which consists of the total undepreciated original costs of capital equipment. Once the agency has concluded what should be total expenses and profit, prices are then set by the company so as to result in revenues not exceeding this allowance. Of course, judgmental elements are part of this process, centrally in determining the reasonable rate of return. But even in profit determination there has been a tendency, as established by example and repetition, to use estimates within a narrow range since they come from publicly accepted sources, such as from accounting compilations of recent earned rates of return of other utility companies. In general the process has centered on the calculation of cost and profit averages from historical accounting data as the basis for future prices. Because of this, the results across price-control agencies have had a tendency to be similar across cases and over time.

The agencies conducting health and safety regulation have developed a process as well. What has evolved over the years in prolonged adversary proceedings are detailed quantitative specifications of equipment or operating conditions. These specifications are easier to certify and enforce than other kinds of standards. They are designed to control indirectly the company's performance as to health conditions, operating safety, or environmental quality. However, in a number of instances, the standards have become the focus of decision-making to such an extent that they have departed widely from performance goals. As with pricing controls, the courts and Congress have had their impact with respect to accountability, and this has resulted in a high degree of specificity in certification of operating practices rather than of the actual health effects in company performance.

The Effects of Regulatory Growth

The spread of regulation is part of the story, as is the regulatory process. But the major concern is with the way in which the commissions have operated and the companies have fared under controls. As might be expected, some individual regulated firms as well as entire regulated industries have performed well from the point of view of the economy as a whole, while others have not done as well as they might have without controls. But in general economic and political conditions in the last ten years have been such that the practices worked out in price and safety regulation have not been able to produce the desired results. Regulation has not added to economy-wide efficiency and growth, as would be the case if prices and service expansion had been in keeping with original goals. In health and safety regulation the invoking of costly equipment standards has not achieved the specific industry results in improved working and living conditions for which they were designed.

The explanation for such results is that those particular practices worked out in case-by-case decision-making did not prove productive in the general economic conditions of the 1970s. Under the inflationary spirals of the late 1960s and early 1970s, agency-allowed annual percentage price increases were smaller and output growth larger than in those industries not subject to price controls. That is, average annual rates of price increase in the regulated utilities fell short of those elsewhere, so that there was significant impetus for more rapid growth in demands for these regulated services. But the increased demands could be satisfied only so long as there was capacity to expand production, and by the middle and late 1970s, with reduced profitability, there was reduced capacity growth. Therefore the growth rate of production fell off from earlier periods more than in the unregulated industries and more than can be attributed to the business cycle. Although some catch up in price increases occurred in the middle 1970s, recessionary conditions during that period put price increases out of phase once again. By the end of the decade, these regulated industries rather than leading in investment and production lagged behind the rest of the economy.

At the same time, those industries most subject to health, safety, and environmental controls began to show larger price and smaller output increases, as if regulation has begun to make production more costly in that sector of the economy. This regulatory pattern may or may not have been adverse or overly costly to the American economy. Given the mandate to eliminate social harms where found, health and safety regulation should have reduced both capacity and production of pollutors and unsafe producers and thereby increased costs of final goods and services. At the same time, then, this regulation should have provided more health and cleaner air. But in general health and safety controls operated in the 1970s in ways that increased costs, increased prices, and reduced production, without improving the quality of work conditions or of the environment. Given the size of price increases and quantity reductions in the most affected industries, and no general benefits, that regulation had a significant adverse effect on the economy.

29

A detailed examination of these economic effects of regulation in recent years is taken up in the following two chapters. The economic impact varied from industry to industry, with some showing significant growth effects under price or environmental controls. But the findings in general are that regulation under inflation and recession has been disastrous for those industries under controls. Given these results, the prospects for industry-by-industry reform of regulatory processes are evaluated in Chapter Four.

2

◇◇◇◇◇

Price and Entry Regulation

Eɴᴀᴄᴛɪɴɢ ʟᴇɢɪsʟᴀᴛɪᴏɴ to establish regulatory commissions is only the beginning. The impact of regulation is largely determined in the first few years of controls by the way an agency translates statutory goals into operating rules. Most of the agencies regulating price and entry had these routines well established by the 1960s. New economic and technological conditions arising in the late 1960s, however, changed the impact of their activities on the regulated companies. This chapter chronicles these results as the movement of the regulated sector from prosperity and growth, and even complacency, to reduced profitability, investment or capacity stringency, and service reductions.

The lesson is that the impact of regulation during the most recent decade has diverged sharply from what was expected when legislation was enacted and operating rules established before the 1960s. To be more precise, practices of administrative agencies which had some positive effects in an era of general economic stability demonstrated great shortcomings in the face of inflationary and recessionary economic conditions. Since disappointing performance of the regulated companies seems to be the result of the interaction between the present control system and these new economic conditions, the system must change before an improvement can take place.

This chapter begins with a description of how price and entry regulation traditionally have been conducted. The common procedures that exist among agencies controlling energy, transportation, and communications companies, noted briefly in Chapter 1, are discussed in more detail and the results from using these processes during the late 1950s and the first half of the 1960s are examined. Then the regulatory responses to new economic conditions that produced the quite different results of the 1965–77 period are evaluated. Finally, the outlook under continued regulation and inflation is described in terms of growth and progress in these industries in the 1980s.

How Price and Entry Regulation Work

Public-utility and other price-regulating commissions, in most instances, have had the power to control all the important decisions of the companies under their jurisdiction. By rule making and case-by-case review, most regulatory agencies in the transportation, energy, and communications sectors decide whether companies operate, the variety and quality of services they can offer, and the structure and level of prices they can charge. Some commissions certify or agree to the purchase of each item of equipment; others review and agree to the fairness of consumer access to service; and a number of commissions carry on reviews of management efficiency. Companies are still free to select production processes and technologies which affect costs; but prices, quantities produced, and even what markets are to be served are determined by the regulators.

As discussed in Chapter 1, there is some commonality across industries, not only in what is regulated but also in how the regulators treat their industries. The usual process begins with certification of a company to provide service in a particular market. For the most part, this prevents the development of additional sources of supply for the same services, but does not restrict competition among substitute products or services. For example, certificate limits are widely imposed on the number of gas companies serving a particular city, but certification does not prevent gas companies from competing with oil and electric companies in the market for household heating. Similarly, certification of entry into interstate trucking does not by itself prevent competition with the railroads in bulk-commodity transportation.

Certification usually involves more than just the number of suppliers, however. Commissions may require regulated companies to provide services they would not otherwise undertake or they may limit company activities by excluding certain types of services. For example, requirements to provide unprofitable rural services have been imposed on transportation, energy, and communications companies in exchange for approval of applications to serve more profitable markets. Agencies may also prevent firms from offering services not directly related to their principal activities. For instance, attempts by telephone companies to provide other communication services and by the railroads to provide trucking services have been disallowed.

In general, certification establishes the dimensions of service in various markets. Regulatory commissions then take the critical next step of determining the level and structure of prices by accepting or rejecting requests by the companies for price increases. Requests are granted if the proposed higher level of revenues does not exceed recent operating costs, depreciation, and a to-be-defined fair return on investment.[1]

The commissions' determinations of what is fair profit may or may not in practice reduce prices below what they would have been in unregulated markets. This result depends on two key profit estimates, that of the amount of investment on which earnings are to be allowed and that of the rate of return on such investment. Commissions generally estimate the investment base from estimates of the original cost less depreciation of that plant and equipment used in the regulated operations. The allowed rates of return come primarily from the judgment of financial and economic experts as to what a company should earn to compete successfully for the funds required for expansion of capacity and ultimately of service to consumers.[2] The importance and the subjective nature of the judgment of the rate of return have together given rise to quite lengthy and detailed proceedings to come to a profit-rate decision.

Because the decision-making process in profit-rate determination is both cumbersome and lengthy, there has been a tendency toward infrequent change and some uniformity across commissions in the results. The New York state regulatory experience provides an illustration of this. During the late 1960s and early 1970s, utilities in New York usually asked for an increase only when their earned rates of return fell substantially below those achieved earlier. Increases requested were larger the lower the recent growth rate in earnings per share and the lower the level of interest coverage (income after taxes divided by total interest charges). Companies also asked for more as the increases allowed other firms under the Public Service Commission's jurisdiction became more generous.[3] While these capital cost factors were important in setting the allowed rate of return, so were the dollar size of the firm's request, the presence of consumer group objections, and subjective evaluation by the regulators of the efficiency of the firm.[4] Since the last three factors changed little during the 1960s, the allowed or fair rates of return also changed little; when they did change adversely to the regulated companies and became more important in the 1970s, the allowed fair profit rates in New York increased but more slowly than did returns on other investments.

Although not all regulatory agencies use these factors in the same way, they generally rely on capital cost estimates and adversary views of these estimates to set narrow limits on the allowed rates of return. They tend to maintain plateaus for long periods of time, with electric, gas, and telephone companies all being granted approximately the same percentage return. When cases cluster during periods of sustained economy-wide inflation, there is a tendency to break through to a higher rate of return level only reluctantly.[5]

The case decisions both at the state and federal levels of regulation in the 1960s and 1970s followed this pattern. Regulation in four industries—electricity, gas retailing, telephone, and airlines—produced few cases in the early 1960s and almost no increase in rates. During the late 1960s and early 1970s, however, the frequency of cases and allowed rates of return both increased, as shown in Table 2.1. Although some commissions consolidated cases, so as to make many rate of return changes with few decisions, the pattern across industries was the same. When small changes in rates of return were the order of the day, cases were few; but when rates increased substantially they did so as a result of a large number of requests put through the regulatory decision process.

Although reluctance to bring cases and agency reluctance to allow increases kept prices constant, they may not have kept prices at that level most appropriate for service development in those industries. The rationale for regulation, the process of regulation, and the economic conditions of the time all played an important role in determining the efficacy of the results. To show effectiveness requires analysis of the process in each phase of the cycles extant from the late 1950s to the late 1970s.

Regulatory Results in the 1950s and Early 1960s

Regulation could produce either (1) lower prices by constraining monopoly power, or (2) the same price level because of ineffective procedures, or (3) higher prices in order to expand investment and capacity so as to provide subsidized services. During the early 1960s, the public-utility and transportation industries showed little price-level effect from regulation. In particular, Thomas Moore found that there had been insubstantial effects on the measurable performance of investor-owned electric utilities.

35

TABLE 2.1 *Cases and Decisions on Revenues*

Industry	Ratios of numbers of case decisions		Average allowed percentage increase in revenues		
	1969/1962	1976/1962	1962	1969	1976
Electricity	1.0	3.3	0.0	1.3	8.8
Gas retailing	0.5	4.9	0.9	0.7	17.6
Telephone	4.0	15.0	0.1	0.9	4.3
Airlines	4.0	6.0	3.0	8.2	11.5

SOURCE: These estimates were compiled from commission and trade association reports for each industry. In the instance of the airlines, industry-wide rate changes were in practice consolidated into one docket at the Civil Aeronautics Board, thus the increase from one docket in 1962 to six in succession over the year 1976.

The hypothetical unregulated price level ranged from 105.7 percent to 97.6 percent of the actual regulated price; that is, some power companies would have charged prices as much as 6 percent higher while other companies would have charged prices 2 percent less had they not been regulated. Raymond Jackson, in another study, found that price controls had not been a significant factor in reducing residential electricity rates in the 1940s or the 1950s. Together with earlier research based both on case and statistical analyses, these studies indicated that regulation was not effective in reducing rates to any great extent before or during the 1950s.[6] Thus it was not possible to tell whether regulation was not using operable procedures as in (2) or was keeping rates on basic local services high to expand other services as in (3).

During the 1960s, however, regulation began to have some price-reducing effect. The commission process became more constraining because companies began requesting increases in rates for the first time in many years, and because those requests were allowed only in part. In particular, after a long period of gains from improved technology and economies of scale, both ceased and the electric companies began to experience rising costs which prompted requests for rate increases. The public-utility commissions responded to these requests with allowances less than the amounts sought, and also tilted the rate structure to favor some groups of consumers.[7]

Telephone regulation, split between state and Federal Communications Commission (FCC) regulation, produced both the rate-level and tilting effects. Because a significant part of total costs was derived from common operations of the national system, an allocation scheme was developed by the regulators to attribute costs to the various types of local and long-distance services. This separations scheme assigned an increasingly larger share of joint costs to interstate long-distance services, thereby allowing the state regulators to hold down increases in residential connection and local usage charges.[8] The resistance to residential rate increases by state commissions kept the level of these charges below even the direct costs of providing some of these services.

An appraisal made of the Illinois Bell Company rate structure in 1967 showed that directly attributable costs were at least twice actual rate levels for local calls but one-sixth of rate levels for long-distance calls. Also, rates that year were below those that an unregulated monopoly company would have set, with the exception of the charges on interstate services.[9] Thus it would appear that regulation was service enhancing since it had kept prices on interstate calls at above-cost levels to provide funds for subsidizing below-cost prices on local service.

The natural-gas pipelines were also subject to split regulatory jurisdiction, since they offered both regulated service to gas retailers and unregulated service to industrial consumers. In the late 1950s and early 1960s, their regulated prices were not significantly lower than unregulated prices, once account had been taken of cost and competitive differences.[10] This was the case even though there were numerous and prolonged regulatory delays in passing on to final buyers the higher field-gas prices of that period. Partly this was the result of the particular regulatory rules used by the Federal Power Commission (FPC). Joint cost allocations took place according to the so-called Atlantic Seaboard Formula, which allocated $(50 + .5x)$ percent of the pipelines' overhead costs to the regulated sector (where x was the percentage of gas sold to retailers). Stanislaw Wellisz showed that application of the formula resulted in a price structure close to that which would have existed in the absence of regulation, because allocations of relatively large proportions of joint costs to regulated sales for rate-setting purposes left the companies with the opportunity to charge relatively high prices on these regulated sales. Wellisz also concluded that the formula was biased against large-volume industrial consumers, raising rates to them and reducing rates to home-heating customers.[11] In applying the formula to individual rate requests, however, the FPC frequently tilted the results to favor the industrial user, thus preventing systematic cross-subsidization according to the formula to home consumers.[12]

Looking across the three industries, generally these studies raise substantial doubts about whether regulation in any significant way reduced the prices set by the natural-gas, electricity, and, to a lesser degree, the telephone companies. With respect to both levels and changes in the structure of rates brought about by regulation in the late 1950s and early 1960s, William Jordan concluded, "If regulation has had any effect it has been limited, slow in developing, and mainly in favor of large consumers."[13]

This state of affairs was the product of the process and formality of commission actions. Early in this period, the companies did not apply for rate increases, given that their costs did not warrant them by commission standards. Indeed, costs per unit of production were generally declining up to 1965, and with or without rate cases, any adjustments were rate reductions. But in the late 1960s, in particular, direct costs were increasing for particular types of services, so that, given company reluctance to bring rate cases, price-cost margins on certain services were substantially reduced. In this sense rate regulation led to the development of rate tilting, intentional or otherwise.

The effects of regulation on rate levels in the transportation industries were somewhat different. Regulatory actions and procedures by the early 1960s had allowed the surface carriers and airlines to raise average fares above levels which would have prevailed in the absence of regulation. Fares without regulation would have been "from 9 to 50 percent lower than they were with regulation, with many differences in the long run exceeding 30 percent."[14] The higher charges, to the extent that company revenues were increased,[15] subsidized certain consumer services or increased the quality of service. Interestingly enough, they did not benefit producers since there is no indication that higher fares resulted in higher profitability. That is, "the evidence is quite inconclusive regarding whether regulation has raised the rate of return for these industries. The railroads were probably helped initially, but regardless of regulation, disinvestment is now painfully taking place in that declining industry. At the same time, with or without regulation, capital is being attracted by the regulated and unregulated airlines and motor carriers sufficient for them to expand equally rapidly in response to increasing demands and advancing technology."[16] The higher fares and rates provided incentives for expanding services, particularly in airline passenger service, so that regulation channeled competition into service quality. In some cases, new services were specifically promoted by the regulatory agencies to such an extent that subsidization of favored consumers reduced regulated firms' overall profits to levels comparable to those in other industries.

The Civil Aeronautics Board achieved these results through the usual rate regulation process, but made two important modifications. First, the CAB set rates on the basis of average industry costs, with the result that in theory the average carrier made zero excess profits, but that each airline not the same as the average would do better or worse. Second, the CAB set rules governing the rate structure that made the profit margin on long-distance roughly one-quarter greater than on short-distance fares. These operating policies were justified on promotional grounds, with the board "attempting to have the airlines use long-haul profits to subsidize short-haul losses.[17] Short-haul markets [were] alleged to be very price elastic because of competition from other modes, and thus the price must be depressed below average cost in order to expand markets. On the other hand, long-haul markets were allegedly less price elastic, making it possible to maintain fares above average costs without losing substantial traffic."[18] This pattern spread widely as the CAB used the fare schedule as the means by which to continue service to small communities as an earlier federal subsidy program to provide service to these communities was scaled down and finally eliminated in the 1950s.[19]

The results from railroad regulation were also along these lines. The case decisions of the Interstate Commerce Commission (ICC) on service and prices in different transportation markets resulted in rates above costs on high-density lines and substantially below costs on light-density feeder-line service to shippers in small communities. In the 1950s, "passenger service, less-than-carload freight service, and agency stations in small towns [were] among the outstanding losing services. . . . One suggested remedy for the deficits from losing services [was] to shift more of this cost burden to freight shippers by increasing carload freight rates."[20] In the 1960s, however, the competition of truck service reduced the tonnage shares on the high-density routes of the Eastern railroads. Faced with either continual reductions in shares or in freight rates, these railroads chose the latter (primarily by not requesting cost-justified rate increases). But charges on light-density lines were also kept level or reduced at the same time, until they were below the direct costs of providing those services. This should have led to accelerated abandonment of light-density lines through regulatory decertification, but regulation slowed down and stopped that process. Thus regulation affected overall profit levels by means of requiring the prolonged continuation of these light-density services.

Trucking regulation was an exception in process, if not in results. In this industry the commissions set limits on profits as a percentage of sales rather than as returns on a rate base, so that constant markups and increased operating costs resulted in higher rates. The rate increases were greatest on services most affected by ICC regulation and least subject to competition from unregulated carriers—for example, on small-volume shipments of merchandise. Working through ICC rate bureaus that forged collective agreement among companies serving the same routes, the regulated highway transportation companies requested higher rates based on higher operating costs, mostly for these less-than-truckload (LTL) shipments of high-quality soft goods. In return for commission approval, there may have been some extension of service offerings to the smaller or less profitable shippers as well, but not with the substantial cross-subsidization results found in rail services.[21]

Was there then a systematic pattern of results from utility and transportation regulation? There were, of course, great differences in the demand and cost conditions faced by each of these industries. The airlines and telephone companies experienced significant demand increases each year, while the railroads had demand reductions, mostly for reasons unrelated to regulation. But, even given these disparities, there was a similarity of results from regulation. Rates in general were not reduced to protect consumers from monopoly pricing. Jordan argued that this result was not simply the failure of the system, but rather was designed to protect the revenues of producers from the vicissitudes of competition.[22] But it was not to the benefit of producers, since rates to home users of natural gas were reduced, access charges to home users of telephones were lowered, and feeder-line charges for railroad and airline services were held down by regulatory policies that benefited some specific classes of consumers. As such, regulation expanded and may even have subsidized the growth of service markets. Regulation may have tipped the balance toward stable and high prices, but it also provided more service for some consumers in the expanding economy of the early 1960s.

Prices and Production under Regulation during the 1960s

During the late 1950s and early 1960s both regulated and unregulated companies experienced price stability and output expansion. Regulated prices crept up slowly during the 1958–61 period, but with annual percentage increases less than those in the unregulated industries (except for airline service, where heavy capital outlays for new equipment justified annual increases of 4 percent or more, as shown in Table 2.2). The price-regulated companies proposed rate increases infrequently during this period, preferring instead to maintain prevailing levels. This could be considered good performance by the regulatory commissions.

During 1961–65, the results were even better, with prices

decreasing slightly under controls. Table 2.2 indicates that prices or rates went down each year on average for each of the six regulated industries, except for motor freight which experienced rate increases of 0.6 percent each year. In contrast, the unregulated service industries, which experienced about the same cost and demand effects from economy-wide business cycle conditions, were increasing prices at about 1.7 percent per year.

Even though the regulated industries seem to have been held to low relative price levels, this need not have been the case. If costs were not increasing in the regulated industries then, even without regulation, prices probably would not have increased. In order to determine whether there was a regulatory effect, raw materials, labor, and capital costs have to be examined in detail. Table 2.2 indicates price changes net of new materials cost changes, since prices in this table are value-added prices (the difference between revenues and material costs per unit of sales). Labor and capital cost changes for the 1961–65 period are given in Table 2.3. Labor costs per unit of sales fell in these industries, so that prices should have decreased. Capital costs came down as well because both interest rates and equity costs for the individual regulated companies over this period followed the downward trend of municipal bond rates from 1958–59 highs to 1963 levels 70 basis points lower.[23] Only for railroads did the price index decrease substantially while costs were not decreasing. But, as mentioned, that is a special case since the shift of high-density traffic to trucking and barge service which was occurring at that time substantially reduced demands for rail service. The rate decreases that took place in the other industries in the early half of the decade were at least in line with cost changes and were not constrained by regulation.

The pattern of price behavior changed substantially in the regulated industries through the rest of the 1960s. During the 1965–69 period, the six regulated industries (shown in Table 2.2) increased their rates or charges from between 0.1 to 2.3 percent per year, with motor freight increases at 2.3 percent twice as large as in any

TABLE 2.2 *Price Behavior in the Regulated Industries, 1958–69*[a]

Industry	1958–61	1961–65	1965–69
	(average annual rates of change in percent)		
Electricity and gas	0.9	−0.1	0.2
Telephone	1.6	−0.5	0.2
Railroad transportation	−3.2	−2.6	1.0
Airline transportation	4.5	−0.7	0.1
Motor freight transportation	0.6	0.6	2.3
Unregulated service industries[b]	1.6	1.7	4.4

[a] Implicit price deflators for gross product originating in sector.

[b] Includes wholesale and retail trade; insurance agents, brokers, services; hotels and other lodging places; personal services; miscellaneous business services; auto repair, services, garages; miscellaneous repair services; motion pictures; amusement, recreation services; educational services.

NOTE: The difference between price changes in regulated and unregulated industries is significant. Statistical regression analyses of these price differences have been done by fitting the equation [annual industry price change $= C_1 + C_2$ year $t + C_3$ industry J] to data for each of the regulated J and unregulated industries for each of the years 1959–61, then 1962–65, and lastly 1966–69. The coefficients C_3 for the regulated industries were all negative and statistically significantly different from zero for the periods 1962–65 and 1966–69 (except for motor freight in 1966–69).

SOURCE: U.S. Department of Commerce, *Workfile 1205-02-02.* 1978 revision.

TABLE 2.3 *Price and Cost Changes in the Regulated Industries, 1961–65*

Industry	Average annual price changes[a] (percent)	Average annual change in unit labor costs[b] (percent)	Average annual change in unit capital costs[c] (percent)
Electricity and gas	−0.1	−0.3	−0.1
Telephone	−0.5	−0.5	−0.1
Railroad transportation	−2.6	−0.8	0.1
Airline transportation	−0.7	−2.6	−3.0
Motor freight transportation	0.6	−0.3	−0.2

[a] Implicit price deflators for gross product originating in sector.
[b] Employee compensation weighted by relative share of total factor cost.
[c] Net interest weighted by relative share of total factor cost.

SOURCE: Calculated from data provided by the U.S. Department of Commerce, *Workfile 1205-02-02*, 1978 revision.

TABLE 2.4 *Price and Cost Changes in the Regulated Industries, 1965–69*

Industry	Average annual price changes [a] (percent)	Average annual change in unit labor costs [b] (percent)	Average annual change in unit capital costs [c] (percent)
Electricity and gas	0.2	0.5	4.1
Telephone	0.2	0.6	3.6
Railroad transportation	1.0	0.8	1.5
Airline transportation	0.1	3.1	5.1
Motor freight transportation	2.3	0.9	1.3

[a] Implicit price deflators for gross product originating in sector.

[b] Employee compensation weighted by relative share of total factor cost.

[c] Net interest weighted by relative share of total factor cost.

SOURCE: Calculated from data provided by the U.S. Department of Commerce, *Workfile 1205-02-02*, 1978 revision.

other regulated industry. But at this time the ten unregulated service industries most similar in market conditions had average price increases of 4.4 percent per year. And this time the regulated rates increased less than regulated industry costs. As Table 2.4 indicates, rate increases were barely equal to labor cost increases, and capital costs went up by several percentage points each year as well. Rates, to keep up with cost changes, should have increased from 2 to 8 percentage points each year.[24] The conclusion is that for the regulated industries in the late 1960s prices were as inflexible upward as they had been downward in the early 1960s.

Another indicator of this change in regulatory price behavior is the fact that margins between sales revenues and operating costs were reduced in 1966–69 from those in the earlier periods (as shown in Table 2.5). Six of the seven regulated industries experienced decreased margins. To the contrary, airline transportation realized only a one point increase in its margin as a result of large increases in service demands which greatly increased capacity utilization.[25]

The question is whether rate regulation determined these changes. If, through increased diligence, regulatory commissions required the companies to keep their rates more in line with costs, so as to reduce profits, then the control system had indeed become more effective. The test is whether the lower sales revenue margins led to reductions in the profitability of investment as measured in returns for investors. There are indeed indications of such profit reductions toward the end of the decade. The regulated companies' rates of return to stockholders and bondholders, as shown in Table 2.6, indicate profits from current and expected future operations (as capitalized in stock price appreciation).[26] In the late 1960s these investors experienced returns much less than those in unregulated industries. Six of the seven regulated industries had returns less than would have been earned by an investor buying the market as a whole. All had returns each year in the 0 to 5 percent range, except for motor freight (which experienced 40 percent returns in 1965 and 1967, and losses in 1966 and 1969,

TABLE 2.5 *Profit Margins on Sales in the Regulated Industries in the 1960s* [a]

Industry	1959–61 (percent)	1962–65 (percent)	1966–69 (percent)
Electricity	45.3	45.2	42.0
Gas transportation	50.8	33.7	22.1
Gas utilities	29.0	27.3	24.4
Telephone	42.5	43.1	40.7
Railroad transportation	26.4	20.4	15.3
Airline transportation	5.7	12.9	14.1
Motor freight transportation	7.4	11.1	1.3
Unregulated service industries	7.2	7.1	7.6

[a] Sales-weighted average of pretax net income after depreciation as a share of sales for years indicated, inclusive. The sample is composed of accounting data on approximately 2,200 firms contained in the Primary, Supplemental, and Tertiary Files, arranged by 4-digit Standard Industrial Classification (SIC) code according to the predominant activity of each firm.

SOURCE: Standard & Poor's Corporation, *Compustat*, September 1978 revision.

TABLE 2.6 *Rates of Return on Investors' Value in the Regulated Industries Compared with the Market Return*[a]

Industry	1962–65		1966–69	
	Actual returns	Difference from expected returns[b]	Actual returns	Difference from expected returns[b]
		(annual percentage rate)		
Electricity	5.8	+0.6	0.6	−4.6
Gas transmission	−0.2	−8.6	4.7	−0.2
Gas utilities	4.9	+0.4	1.6	−3.5
Telephone	2.4	−2.9	0.2	−5.0
Railroad transportation	8.4	+2.6	1.8	−3.3
Airline transportation	24.1	+17.4	1.4	−3.7
Motor freight transportation	18.2	+7.4	8.9	+4.6
Market return	8.2		5.0	

[a] Return on investors' value for a given industry is the market value-weighted average of all interest and dividends plus price appreciation divided by the market value of all securities for that industry.

[b] Expected returns on investors' value are derived by adjusting for the industry-specific risk premium (the BETA required by investors). The BETA adjustment process is explained in Appendix D.

SOURCE: See Table 2.5.

because of large swings in operating rates and thus in profit margins on sales). On the whole, investors were realizing less rate of return on the shares of regulated companies than on those of comparable companies elsewhere in the economy.

Returns declined most likely because of rising costs and because of the upward inflexibility of regulated prices. In some cases, as well, changes occurring in regulation affected the value of investments in these industries. For example, telephone investment prospects were affected by a Federal Communications Commission investigation which subjected rates of return on long-distance telephone service to a full formal review for the first time. This reduced stockholders' estimates of future profitability, thereby causing telephone company stock prices to fall so as to decrease returns on investors' value. More generally, however, the difference in regulation was that in this period of rising costs it had become necessary to apply for rate increases. Whether application was sooner or later, the combination of company reluctance, regulatory lag, and commission decisions held down profit margins.

This kind of regulatory effectiveness can as a matter of course bring about changes in investment and production beneficial to the economy as a whole. Regulation that reduces prices and profitability has a positive effect when profits are brought into line with capital costs, and when investment and production then expand to meet the increased demand attendant upon lower price levels. But the process is not beneficial when regulated rates of return fall below capital costs so that investment and production are reduced while demands for service increase.

Both results probably occurred in the transportation and public-utility industries in the late 1960s. As shown in Table 2.7, investment growth rates were not generally increased by reduced stockholders' profitability during the second half of the decade. Investment increased in some but decreased in other industries, but a good part of these changes also took place because of differing prospects for demand growth. With good prospects in electricity

TABLE 2.7 *Annual Rates of Real Investment in the Regulated Industries* [a]

Industry	1958–61	1961–65	1965–69
	(average annual rate of change in percent)		
Electricity	–4.2	5.4	15.3
Gas	–1.4	2.6	7.5
Telephone	6.3	10.8	7.2
Railroad transportation	–2.3	23.8	–4.9
Airline transportation	24.9	12.7	16.0
Motor freight transportation	5.1	22.9	–0.3
Unregulated service industries	6.2	8.5	1.0

[a] Real gross private investment.

SOURCE: U.S. Department of Labor (unpublished data, 1978) and Data Resources, Incorporated.

and airlines for increased service demand, these industries had high investment growth, while poor prospects in railroad and overextended investment earlier in trucking kept investment in these sectors low. This is to say that, given prospective returns more or less the same as prospective costs of capital, regulation probably did not systematically affect investment decisions during the late 1960s. As shown in Table 2.8, GNP growth rates in the regulated industries also did not change because of the constraints keeping prices down when they were rising in other industries. Sales growth exceeded that in the unregulated service industries, except for railroad transportation, although this rate of growth did decline slightly in three of these industries. Thus regulation seems to have operated so as to allow the companies to meet rapidly growing demands in markets while the high demand growth was in part stimulated by the relatively low rate of regulated price increase.

Some regulated companies began to find limits on meeting expanded regulatory service requirements, however, and service quality generally declined in these industries. In particular, the railroads experienced a narrowing of price-cost margins, low profitability, declining investment, and as a result widespread cutbacks in service offerings in low-density markets. To be sure, this supply scenario was not entirely the result of regulation, but reduced margins were the product of the regulatory process of controlling exit from sparsely used lines. There was also the case of natural-gas-field-price regulation. As the next section indicates, regulation there reduced prices so far below unregulated levels that shortages of gas resulted.

The Exceptional Case of Regulation of Natural-Gas-Field Prices

During the 1960s the Federal Power Commission (FPC) conducted an extensive effort to regulate the prices at which pro-

TABLE 2.8 *Production Changes in the Regulated Industries* [a]

Industry	1958–61	1961–65	1965–69
	(average annual rate of change in percent)		
Electricity and gas	7.3	5.3	6.5
Telephone	6.3	8.7	9.3
Railroad transportation	0.8	5.3	0.5
Airline transportation	6.3	14.1	13.9
Motor freight transportation	5.8	7.4	5.5
Unregulated service industries	3.7	5.5	4.2

[a]Real gross product originating in sector.

SOURCE: See Table 2.2.

ducers sell natural gas to interstate pipelines. Given that most deliveries went to these pipelines, this regulation was effective in holding down field prices on both local and interstate sales. The resulting price freeze led to extensive increases in retail demands for gas and, eventually, to decreases in supplies going into the pipelines. Inevitably there developed a substantial shortage of natural gas. This in turn produced complicating problems throughout the energy industries: more rapid extraction of gas from reserves; shifting of new supplies to unregulated intrastate customers instead of to the interstate pipelines; and, consequently, the switching from gas to oil in interstate markets thereby increasing imports of foreign fuel by the middle 1970s.

These regulatory effects were not surprising given the methods used by the commission. Wellhead regulation was initiated by the FPC after the Supreme Court held in 1954 that the commission had the responsibility to control prices on sales by gas-field producers to the interstate pipelines.[27] Prior to this, there had been considerable controversy about whether regulation extended to field pricing and the FPC had not set limits on producers' prices. But with Congress unable to provide a bill granting a clear producer exemption, and with the 1954 court decision that required the FPC to hold the line on price, the commission in the late 1950s finally began to establish means of controlling new contract prices. Its first approach was to treat each producer as a public utility and to set prices on the basis of individual company costs of service, including operating costs, depreciation, and fair return. After some years of trying this approach, it became apparent that the sheer volume of cases involving thousands of transactions and producers made the case-by-case approach unwieldy.

The second approach was to set regional price ceilings and to restrict all individual producers within a region to transaction prices no higher than the ceilings. To accomplish this, the FPC in 1960 divided the Southwest into five geographical areas, set interim ceiling prices at the 1960 levels for new contracts, and began hearings to determine the final ceiling prices for each area.

Through the 1960s, agency decisions and court reviews resulted in permanent price limits only for the Permian Basin of West Texas and for Southern Louisiana. At the close of the decade, the process had not yet been completed for other areas, but the interim ceiling prices and the two sets of permanent maximum prices had set a pattern for price controls for the entire Southwest gas-producing region. The first proceeding set prices for the Permian Basin only slightly higher than the interim 1960 prices, and the second proceeding set prices for Southern Louisiana at the interim 1960 level.[28] The pattern had been established that the interim ceilings which reproduced transactions prices of the late 1950s were to be the allowed prices for the full decade of the 1960s.

That the commission meant to hold the price line was evident, not only from the *de facto* freeze but also from the way in which price structures were specified in the decisions. The commission set two price levels in the initial area rate proceedings, with higher prices on new gas (recently discovered and developed, but not yet committed to a specific buyer) and lower prices on old gas (already committed to a buyer). This practice was extended by detailed proceedings to determine whether the new gas price would be high enough to cover the cost of developing those additional supplies. This two-price system indicated that the commission wanted to prevent prices from increasing without causing significant supply shortages. But this was impossible to achieve. The way that the proceedings worked in practice required that the regulated price ceilings for both the old and the new gas be based on previous prices. As costs increased, prices lagged behind and shortages had to appear.

Intent was shown by basing the allowed returns on average historical costs of developing established supplies. Thus, in the Permian Basin Case, the commission's staff surveyed the operating gas producers in order to find their costs of production for the base year of 1960. Experts employed by the producers and the retail distributors made separate surveys, and together the staff and producer studies provided a range of estimates of historical exploration and development costs per unit of new and old gas delivered into a pipeline. After considerable appraisal of these estimates, the FPC set price ceilings in the middle of these estimates of historical average costs.

What this process did was to allow price ceilings roughly equal to the interim prices set in the early 1960s. In the Permian Basin case, for example, the commission set a new gas price ceiling at approximately 16.5 cents per thousand cubic feet (MCF) while the interim ceilings had been close to 16 cents up to that time. That the final ceiling prices equaled the provisional prices was not simply chance. The provisional price ceilings themselves determined the development activity which produced the historical costs which in turn determined the final prices. In other words, if producers in the early 1960s surmised that they were unlikely to be able to sell gas at much more than the interim prices, then they developed only those reserves having costs lower than these interim prices. This resulted in the average cost of new reserves being roughly equal to the interim ceilings (given no significantly good or ill fortune in development). Thus using these recent historical average costs to set future average prices was in effect using historical prices to set future prices.[29]

Fixing the future price of gas in 1960 dollars resulted in a gas price which was lower than comparable oil and coal prices at most major consuming points. This had the effect of increasing demand for gas compared to other fuels. The implementation of new environmental standards also increased the demand for gas relative to other fuels, principally because of its clean burning characteristics. As customers switched to gas and obtained connections to pipelines or retailers, the pipelines sought more contracted supplies to meet the higher expected consumption draughts on their systems. Although the pipelines sought the customary fifteen-year reserve backing for each annual increment of production delivery, they failed to obtain these amounts. In fact, had the fifteen-year backing been granted, the total new commitments of producers to the interstate pipelines each year would have to have been 21 to 24 trillion cubic feet. However, commitments were in fact in the range of 9 to 16 trillion cubic feet in the late 1960s. Thus demand was increasing at such a rate as to create reserve-backing shortages under ceiling price regulation, shortages which were realized in the form of reduced reserves available for guaranteeing future service to established customers.

This reserve gap would not have occurred had new-contract field prices been higher. There is no way to be sure how much prices would have had to increase beyond ceiling levels to bring forth sufficient supply and to reduce demand for reserves so as to eliminate the shortage. But prices 50 percent greater than regulated levels over the period 1968–72 would probably have brought forth more than a trillion cubic feet of additional reserves committed to the interstate pipelines each year. And passing such price increases on to final consumers would have curtailed their consumption growth by more than one-half a trillion cubic feet. Together these changes would have reduced the rundown of reserves, as shown in Table 2.9, by adding to reserve development and reducing production rates, so that immediate manifestations of shortages would have disappeared.

Because such price increases were not allowed, the reserve depletion continued. Low prices particularly added to the production demands from new customers, and to satisfy them, producers had to provide gas for current consumption from existing committed reserves. This could continue for only a few years; thus by 1972 there were not enough committed reserves to allow production to meet all current demands and operating shortages began to occur.

Production shortages brought about another significant change in the regulatory process. In order to prevent disruptions from interrupted service, the FPC created priority rankings for customers which limited access to gas and required those on the low priority schedule to use other fuels during certain periods. Thus the result of price controls in the 1960s was rationing in the 1970s.

TABLE 2.9 *Gas-Field Production and Demand, 1968–72*

Year	Annual reserve additions	Annual production	Hypothetical unregulated[a] reserve additions	Hypothetical unregulated production
		(trillions of cubic feet)		
1968	19.3	19.9	19.6	19.6
1969	17.8	21.3	18.7	20.4
1970	15.1	22.6	16.3	21.1
1971	14.4	22.8	15.9	22.0
1972	15.3	23.3	16.8	22.7

[a] Unregulated production and reserves are derived from simulation of market response to a price series approximately twice the level of regulated prices. An econometric model of regional natural gas supplies and wholesale demand was used for the simulations. The model is described in P. W. MacAvoy and R. S. Pindyck, *The Economics of the Natural Gas Shortage* (Rotterdam, North-Holland Press, 1975).

These results from regulation could not have been avoided as long as the commission was in control. The sequence of reserve depletion, production shortage, and rationing can in fact be predicted from the commission's control practices. Regulation of a depleting reserve that for workability sets prices based on average costs rather than on the high costs of expanding supplies necessarily sets prices below levels at which additional supplies match expanding demands. Practices that use historical costs for current price-level determination when current costs are higher have to set prices too low. These effects were masked in the short term by increased production out of already committed reserves. Only when such inventory depletion became severe did shortages of production begin to appear. In most regulated industries, this would have happened sooner and the results would have been clearer. By the time the gas shortage arrived, it was too late to recognize and adjust, and more regulation had become necessary to allocate the shortage among consumers.

Price Regulation during the Late 1960s and 1970s

The economic conditions that made the natural-gas industry the exception in the early 1960s spread to the other price-regulated industries in the late 1960s and early 1970s. To be sure, the cost conditions of field-gas supply were rather special. Exploration and development costs increased each year, always making costs of additional supply greater than the average costs and prices for this resource. But in the late 1960s similar cost patterns began to appear in the other energy industries and in transportation and communications. Cost of materials and construction went up from 5 to 10 percent, which increased cost of current supply to levels higher than historical average costs. As in the natural-gas industry, the regulated price-setting process in these other industries continued to hold price levels close to historical average costs. Thus changes in prices failed to provide compensation for the higher costs of expanding service and the first stages of shortage conditions began to appear in the form of reduced investment, capacity, and production growth. Such conditions occurred at a different time and to a different degree in each of these industries. On the whole, however, overregulation dominated the commissions and companies in the energy industries and in transportation and communications in the early 1970s.

Cost increases were much more substantial than in the earlier decade. Wholesale prices from 1970 through 1976 increased by more than 60 percent for all commodities, and by almost 70 percent for the materials important in the production of manufactured goods. At the same time unit labor costs increased by more than 40 percent, in part because of reduced rates of productivity growth. High productivity growth rates had been realized because of the economies of scale inherent in rapid capacity growth, but such economies had come to an end with reduced capacity growth during the cyclical downturns of 1970 and 1974–75. Larger still was the 160 percent increase in wholesale fuel prices over that period caused by the OPEC price hikes during 1973–76.[30] This sustained input-factor-cost increase greatly increased prices in the industries providing materials to the regulated companies.

With materials, labor, and fuel cost increases outstripping previous levels, the appropriate policy for regulated companies would have been to request and put into effect substantial price increases. Nevertheless, even though many more requests were made and granted, substantial rate increases were not put into effect. Rates and fares increased on average by 2 to 4 percent per year during 1969–73 for the public utilities and by 4 to 7 percent per year for the transportation industries (as shown in Table 2.10). Only in the middle 1970s after accumulated higher capital and materials costs had raised average historical costs did the actual rates increase substantially.

Price-level changes in these six regulated industries were not sufficient to maintain profit margins—five of the six industries had lower margins than in 1966–69 (as shown in Tables 2.5 and

TABLE 2.10 *Price Behavior in the Regulated Industries, 1969–77* [a]

Industry	1969–73	1973–77
	(average annual rates of change in percent)	
Electricity and gas	4.3	11.3
Telephone	2.5	2.9
Railroad transportation	7.2	8.6
Airline transportation	6.0	7.9
Motor freight transportation	3.6	5.7
Unregulated service industries	4.7	7.8

[a] Implicit price deflators for gross product originating in sector.

NOTE: As for previous periods as shown in Table 2.2, the regression equations ($\Delta p/p = C_1 + C_2 Y_t + C_3 I_j$) have been fitted for the periods 1970–73 and 1974–77, with Δp the percentage price change in each industry, Y_t the observation for year t, and I_j the regulated industry j. The coefficients for I_j in the 1970–73 regression were negative only for electricity, telephone, and motor freight and all were statistically insignificant. The coefficients for I_j in the 1974–77 regressions were negative only for telephone and motor freight and only the coefficient for telephones was significant.

SOURCE: See Table 2.2.

2.11). On the whole, the regulated sector did worse during the 1970s than other industries, with the public utilities, railroads, and later the airlines experiencing margin declines while unregulated service companies experienced no such general margin declines.

This is indicated further by differences between the behavior of regulated companies where they operated under controls and similar companies or operations outside of controls. Although public utilities and common-carrier transportation companies have long been regulated, they may still provide some services that are not controlled by a regulatory agency. For example, gas sales by the interstate pipelines directly to industry have not been regulated. More important, some companies in these industries have not been regulated at all for various reasons. Some municipal power companies and intrastate airlines, for example, have not been subject either to state or to national commission jurisdiction. The experience of these companies in nonregulated markets under the inflationary conditions of the 1970s shows the inflexibility of regulated prices. Table 2.12 shows that regulated prices went down less in the 1960s, but also generally increased less in the early 1970s than unregulated rates in the three industries for which there is information. In the later period, electric-power and natural-gas prices in unregulated markets increased at twice the rate of those in regulated markets, as could be expected from the rapid increase in costs in the late 1960s. Unregulated airline fares in Texas and California, in particular, were much more in line with cost changes than the regulated interstate fares, decreasing more in the early 1960s but increasing more after 1965. These unregulated fares began to increase in the 1965–69 period, at 2 percent per annum, while regulated fares were still going down. They were increasing at a 12 percent annual rate by the middle 1970s while regulated fares were increasing only at a 7 percent rate. To be sure, particular market conditions could have caused unregulated rates to increase earlier, and by larger amounts, in some industries than in others. But, in general, regulated rates

TABLE 2.11 *Profit Margins on Sales in the Regulated Industries in the 1970s* [a]

Industry	1970–73 (percent)	1974–77 (percent)
Electricity	33.2	29.3
Gas transportation	24.4	24.3
Gas utilities	22.2	20.4
Telephone	33.3	34.1
Railroad transportation	14.7	13.4
Airline transportation	5.5	6.6
Motor freight transportation	10.4	9.6
Unregulated service industries	6.8	7.4

[a] Sales-weighted average of pretax net income after depreciation as a share of sales for years indicated, inclusive. The sample is composed of accounting data on approximately 2,200 firms contained in the Primary, Supplemental, and Tertiary Files, arranged by 4-digit Standard Industrial Classification (SIC) code according to the predominant activity of each firm.

SOURCE: Standard & Poor's Corporation, *Compustat*, September 1978 revision.

TABLE 2.12 *Price Changes in Regulated and Unregulated Service*

Industry	1961–65	1965–69	1969–73 (annual average rates of change in percent)	1973–most recent year
Electricity				
1. Privately owned classes A and B (regulated)	−1.8	−1.4	+5.6	+22.4 (1975)
2. Municipally owned unregulated electric utilities	−6.2	−2.0	+10.1	+10.4 (1975)
Natural gas				
1. Regulated sales for resale	0.0	−0.1	+6.4	+26.6 (1976)
2. Unregulated mainline industrial sales of major interstate pipelines	+0.6	+0.1	+11.8	+33.8 (1976)
Airlines				
1. Regulated interstate routes	+4.2	−3.3	+4.8	+6.8 (1976)
2. Unregulated intrastate routes	−1.1	+2.2	+4.0	+11.8 (1976)

TABLE 2.12 (Continued)

SOURCES:

Electricity: For privately owned utilities, various editions of *Statistics of Privately Owned Electric Utilities in the United States* (FPC).

For unregulated municipally owned electric utilities, various editions of *Statistics of Publicly Owned Electric Utilities in the United States* (FPC). The same methodology was to select larger, vertically integrated municipal utilities. The sample varies from year to year because data were not reported for certain years. Weighted average price changes were based on total electrical operating revenue per 1,000 kwh sales.

Natural Gas: For regulated sales for resale, various editions of *Gas Facts* (American Gas Association). For mainline industrial sales of major interstate gas pipeline companies; *Statistics of Interstate Natural Gas Pipeline Companies 1976* (Energy Information Administration, Department of Energy). Weighted averages for 1976 were based on revenue and volume data which includes a small fraction of field sales as well as mainline sales.

Airlines: For interstate airline fares, data were collected on three interstate routes: Chicago/New York, Chicago/Kansas City, New York/Miami (+Fort Lauderdale). Weighted average price changes were based on one-way coach fares before taxes. Source for fares: Reuben H. Donnelly Corporation, *Official Airline Guide: North American Quick Reference Editions* (January issues, 1961–76). Source for passenger-mile data: *Domestic Origin-Destination Survey of Airline Passenger Traffic* (CAB). Weights for the 1961–67 period were based on "All or Part Coach" seat-miles which included discounts. Weights for the 1968–71 period were based only on seat-miles in the full-fare coach category. (The *Origin-Destination Survey* did not list seat-mile data separately for discounts until 1968.) Problems of comparability are presented by the change in compilation methods which the *Origin-Destination Survey* underwent in 1968, from true origin-destination to directional origin-destination.

The four selected intrastate routes are: Dallas/Houston, Los Angeles/San Francisco, Los Angeles/San Diego, and San Diego/San Francisco. Weighted average price changes were based on one-way coach fares before taxes. Sources for intrastate data: Pacific Southwest Airlines; Southwest Airlines; Simat, Helliesen and Eichner, Inc., *An Analysis of the Intrastate Air Carrier Regulatory Forum*, vol. 2, Technical Report, III-30 (January 1976); Reuben H. Donnelly Corporation, *Official Airline Guide: North American Quick Reference Editions* (January issues, 1961–76).

TABLE 2.13 *Rates of Return in the Regulated Industries in the 1970s*

Industry	Return on investors' value		Difference between actual returns and expected returns[a]	
	1970–73	1974–77	1970–73	1974–77
	(percent)		(percent)	
Electricity	3.8	8.3	− 1.2	+ 2.4
Gas transportation	6.8	9.7	+ 2.6	+ 3.9
Gas utilities	5.4	10.9	+ 0.5	+ 5.0
Telephone	5.6	8.7	+ 0.6	+ 2.8
Railroad transportation	8.3	6.0	+ 3.4	+ 0.1
Airline transportation	1.0	5.0	− 3.6	− 0.9
Motor freight transportation	8.2	7.9	+ 4.6	+ 2.2
Market return	4.3	5.8		

[a] See notes *a* and *b* in Table 2.6.
SOURCE: See Table 2.5.

were kept down beginning in the late 1960s when inflationary demand and cost conditions otherwise would have caused them to increase, as evidenced by unregulated market price behavior under highly similar market conditions.

These pricing conditions had an impact on the profitability of regulated companies and, consequently, on their investment and service growth.[31] The regulated companies had already experienced substantial reductions in relative rates of return to stockholders in the latter half of the 1960s, as evidenced by returns on their shares relative to the market. Investors' rates of return stayed close to the disappointingly low market rates of 4 percent per annum in the 1970–73 period, with electricity and airline below and only railroad returns above this level (as shown in Table 2.13). These returns also were disappointing because of the size of the decrease. Returns on airline holdings fell from 24 percent per annum in 1962–65 to 1 percent in 1966–69 and in 1970–73, and returns on both railroad and trucking investments in 1970–73 were from one-third to one-half those in the early 1960s (see Tables 2.6 and 2.13). These decreases were greater than those attributable to low returns in the market generally (as shown in Table 2.14), since returns in five of the seven industries were below the market profit rate over the entire period.

Because of the depressing effects of regulation on profitability, annual real net investment in these industries began to decline in the early 1970s (see Table 2.15). The three transportation industries realized no more than half as much investment as in the late 1960s, and gas-transportation-equipment expenditures were greatly reduced as well. There were declines in investment rates in the electricity industry of one-third; and the telephone industry continued its relatively low 7 percent rates of the late 1960s rather than the 11 percent rate of the earlier half of the 1960s. On the whole, investment was not substantially greater in the regulated industries than in industry and trade, even though that had been the case in earlier decades.

Effects on production of reduced investment were not long in

TABLE 2.14 *Return on Investors' Values in the Regulated Industries, 1966–73*

Industry	Actual returns on investors' value [a]	Expected returns on investors' value (percent)	Difference between actual returns and expected returns
Electricity	2.2	5.1	− 2.9
Gas transportation	5.8	4.6	+ 1.2
Gas utilities	3.5	5.0	− 1.5
Telephone	2.9	5.1	− 2.2
Railroad transportation	5.0	5.0	+ 0.0
Airline transportation	1.2	4.8	− 3.6
Motor freight transportation	8.5	4.2	+ 4.3
Market return	4.8		

[a] See notes *a* and *b* in Table 2.6.
SOURCE: See Table 2.5.

TABLE 2.15 *Investment and Production Growth in the Regulated Industries*

Industry	Real net investment		Real GNP growth		
	1965–69	1969–73	1965–69	1969–73	1973–77
	(average annual rates of change in percent)				
Electricity	15.3	9.7	6.5[a]	4.6[a]	0.1[a]
Gas	7.5	−3.1	6.5[a]	4.6[a]	0.1[a]
Telephone	7.2	7.7	9.3	8.2	7.5
Railroad transportation	−4.9	−2.7	0.5	−1.3	−3.8
Airline transportation	16.0	−5.3	13.9	4.8	2.6
Motor freight transportation	−0.3	3.1	5.5	7.3	2.1
Unregulated service industries	1.0	2.6	4.2	4.7	2.1

[a] Electricity and gas combined.

NOTE and SOURCE: See Tables 2.7 and 2.8.

appearing. As indicated in Table 2.15, the 1970s GNP growth rates in these industries were from 2 to 15 percentage points less than in the late 1960s. This was concomitant with, and at least partially the result of, a slowdown in GNP growth for the economy as a whole (there was a reduction in the average annual GNP growth rate in the unregulated industries of 2 percentage points over the ten years as well). But the reduction in growth rates was greater in almost all of the regulated industries, causing this sector to fall from its leading position to production growth rates roughly the same as those in other sectors.

The regulatory effects on the quality of service were as important and in the same direction. The original rationale for regulatory controls, once prices had been brought down from monopoly levels, was for the commissions to push the regulated industries to higher levels of provision of service than would have occurred with open and uncontrolled pricing in these markets. But the economic conditions of the 1970s caused the pressures and incentives for service expansion to decline greatly. With prices held down while costs increased, service quality was reduced. Indices of service quality for these industries (shown in Table 2.16) demonstrate these effects. Although incomplete and extremely crude, the ratios of quality indicate that frequency, reliability, or availability of services either declined or failed to improve in many of the regulated industries in the last half of the 1960s and the early 1970s. The original mandate for licensing common carriers and for price-setting to expand market coverage had been allowed to lapse during the decade.

Why these results? Two distinct regulatory processes substantially controlled the regulated companies during these economic conditions of the 1970s. Regulatory lag began to work against rather than for these companies, and the commissions restrained current-dollar rate increases.[32] When costs were falling but rates were kept constant in the late 1950s, regulatory lag was to the advantage of the regulated firm because profits continued to increase until such time as the commission forced service increases or

TABLE 2.16 Service Quality in the Regulated Industries

Industry	$\dfrac{\text{1961 index}}{\text{1958 index}}$	$\dfrac{\text{1965 index}}{\text{1958 index}}$	$\dfrac{\text{1969 index}}{\text{1958 index}}$	$\dfrac{\text{1973 index}}{\text{1958 index}}$	$\dfrac{\text{Index, most recent year}}{\text{1958 index}}$
Electricity	1.46	1.08	0.78	0.98	1.62 (1976)
Natural gas	0.90	0.93	0.63	0.44	0.41 (1975)
Telephones	0.93	0.96	0.82	0.82	0.94 (1977)
Railroads	1.02	1.12	1.10	1.08	0.93 (1976)
Airlines	1.14	1.16	1.29	1.25	1.15 (1976)
Trucks	0.96	0.95	0.77	1.02	1.05 (1976)

NOTE: For all industries in the table above, a ratio of less than unity represents a decline in the service-quality index, whereas a ratio greater than unity represents an improvement. All ratios are expressed in decimal form, not as percentages.

SOURCES: Service Quality Indices

Electricity: gross reserve/peak demand ratio for electricity in the U.S.
SOURCE: National Electric Reliability Council for 1961–76; see also the FPC, *Annual Report* (Washington, D.C.: U.S. Government Printing Office, 1958).

Natural gas: reserve/production ratio of interstate natural gas supply.
SOURCE: FPC *Annual Reports* (various editions).

Telephones: inverse of "Customer Reports Per 100 Stations."
SOURCE: Customer Trouble Report Summary (E-2700), AT&T.

Railroads: inverse of turnaround time, average all cars (in days), Class I Railroads.
SOURCE: ICC, *Annual Reports* (Washington, D.C.: U.S. Government Printing Office, 1958–1976).

Airlines: ratio of empty/total available seats, domestic trunk airlines.
SOURCE: Civil Aeronautics Board staff data compilations.

Trucks: freight claim experience, as measured by freight revenue/cargo loss and damage insurance for Class I and Class II General Freight Common Carriers, Intercity, Total U.S.
SOURCE: *Trincs Blue Book of the Trucking Industry,* various editions.

reductions in rates. When costs began to rise, however, as they did in the late 1960s, regulatory lag worked against the firm since its historical costs for rate setting were falling behind current costs.[33] The difference between historical and current costs widened as the increase in the number of rate applications extended the amount of time required for case decisions. Thus the greater the inflation, and the longer the lag in deciding on increases in regulated prices, the greater the profit reduction effect of controls on these industries.

Beyond the problems of regulatory lag, rate increases, when granted, were not as substantial relative to cost increases as they had been earlier. One reason for this was that, to avoid adverse public reactions, rate-setting agencies would not grant price increases that were very large in billions of dollars. The dollar sizes of proposed additional revenues so concerned regulators that they became reluctant to grant even those increases that were fully justified by the cost-based criteria which had been acceptable previously.

Both regulatory lag and this money illusion were important in setting limits on price changes. Cost factors, such as in operating expenses and capital, could no longer by themselves explain actual rate changes.[34] The rate increases granted during the late 1960s were on average five quarters behind cost changes. In the transportation sector the allowed increases eventually caught up to cost changes because regulated prices there increased by somewhat more than the current cost changes by the middle 1970s. In electricity, large gaps between cost and price changes occurred in the late 1960s, but in gas transportation the squeeze came later when contracts with utilities failed to pass through the higher field prices put into effect in the middle 1970s.[35] In both industries, where pressures from fuel price increases were most severe, regulatory lag and money illusion resulted in price increases below cost increases through the 1970s.

The contrast between the earlier and the more recent results from regulation could not be greater. In the 1960s the lower rates

72

of price increase were accompanied by higher rates of production and real GNP increase in the regulated industries. But in the first half of the 1970s the lower rates of price increase under regulation were accompanied by reduced rates of investment and production increase. The reason is that the latter-period price changes did not compensate for cost increases, so that profitability and capacity additions were reduced and ultimately production growth had to be cut back. In fact, output increases were reduced by one-half to two-thirds of the change in these same regulated industries in the previous decade so that for the first time growth was no greater there than in the unregulated sector of the economy.

The reduced rates of output growth in energy, transportation, and communications have been a widely noted and explained phenomenon. Of the many reasons given for this behavior, the most likely appears to be that lower output growth was in line with a marked slowdown in investment in these industries. Companies had become reluctant to initiate new service and were much slower in improving service. In the extreme cases, actual capacity limits were reached which prevented the companies from extending service to new customers. These conditions slowed GNP growth in the energy, transportation, and communications industries in ways that replicated the first dampening effects of price controls in the gas industry in the late 1960s. In this sense, the earlier gas case exception in regulation became the later rule.

Conditions and Prospects for the Regulated Industries in the Late 1970s.

The results of a decade of regulatory lag and reluctance to allow rate increases have begun to appear in all of these industries. But the extent has differed from industry to industry, depending on the size of cost increases and the severity of regulation. In those with significant energy and capital cost hikes and recalcitrant commissions, shortages of capacity and production have been in the offing. In contrast, the industries still able to bring forth substantial cost reductions have not been much held back by regulatory delays and rejections.

The poor results and prospects are exemplified by conditions in the electric power industry. Retail prices for electricity in most cases were regulated in the 1970s by state public-utility commissions in an especially time-consuming and backward-looking process. When faced with sharply increased construction and operating costs together with doubled interest rates, most of the power companies requested rate increases at much the same time. The commissions thus faced a greatly increased number of revenue and cost reviews, from an average of 4 per year during 1964–68 to 53 in 1972 and 56 in 1973. The time required for a decision consequently increased from roughly 8 months to 2 years. With the lengthening of the interval from request to when increased rates went into effect, rates and charges fell behind costs.

But even more than the delays, the decisions from the case process significantly reduced the earnings of electric power companies. In cases in 31 states in 1974, the commissions allowed an average rate of return of 8.2 percent (which included 83 percent of what was requested). But capital costs were rising rapidly. Interest rates which in 1970 had been 8.8 percent had risen to 9.7 percent in June 1974 (in response to federal fiscal and monetary policies designed to cut back on monetary and credit growth). But in cases decided in 39 states as late as 1976, only an 8.8 percent rate of return was allowed (only 51 percent of that requested).

Higher interest rates combined with such price regulation in fact reduced earned returns on stockholders' equity from 12 to 15 percent in the late 1960s to between 10 and 11 percent in 1974. The difference between the rate of return on equity and the current average interest rate on long-term debt, which had been nearly 8 percentage points in 1964, fell to little more than 2 percentage points in the middle 1970s. With the spread between debt and equity returns to compensate for the risk of equity investment virtually eliminated, equity investment was no longer attractive.[36]

74

At this point capital stringency began to reappear. In the middle 1970s, further investments from stockholders were restricted as electric utility stock prices fell to about 75 percent of the book value of existing investments. With little hope of obtaining further equity capital, the power companies had to issue new debt. But because of regulatory limits on the debt-equity ratio, sufficient capital to expand generating capacity could not be raised through further debt issues either. As a consequence, capacity to produce electricity did not increase rapidly. By holding allowed returns to less than current equity and debt costs, the regulatory commissions began the process of cutting back investment, reducing the growth of generating capacity, and finally reducing production in the electric-power industry. This is a long process affecting each company differently, depending on individual costs of fuel and capital and on rates of growth in demand. The results have not been current shortages, since an investment cutback takes ten years to be realized in reduced capacity levels. But in the coming decade, electricity appears to be headed for investment and production shortfalls from current rate-of-return controls.[37]

The airline industry could show the same results over the same period. With sustained, high-level economic growth, passenger demand should increase substantially. Whether this leads to expanded service, or to deterioration of existing service levels, depends on how regulation operates in the future. Most important, recent reductions in regulation could determine by themselves what is likely to take place. The airlines, in their first reaction to regulation and inflation, reduced service quality significantly in the early 1970s. After increasing investment by 16 percent from 1965 to 1969, the domestic airlines cut back capital outlays by 5 percent in the 1969–73 period, and by 25 percent in the 1973–77 period. This might have been expected because of excess capacity in the late 1960s as a result of overly optimistic forecasts of both demand and fare increases. But investment cutbacks, beyond merely reducing excess capacity, reduced service-quality levels as well. This is shown by the 10 percent decline in the airline-service quality index from 1969 to 1973, and the 6 percent further decline from 1973 to 1977 (as shown in Table 2.16). Throughout this period, as traffic grew, the number of flights declined and airline passengers were offered less convenient scheduling and more crowded flights each year during the ten years after the new jets were put into operation. The thrust of CAB regulation toward an expansive airline system had been brought to a stop.

This state of affairs could very well extend into the 1980s. Comparisons of projected airframe replacement and expansion expenditures to meet service demands with the required level of cash flow to finance such expenditures indicate that the regulated airlines may not be able to obtain sufficient financial resources. More than 1,400 fleet additions requiring roughly $19 billion of capital expenditures will be required to attain a 6 percent annual growth rate in available passenger-miles by 1988. But only some $6 billion would be forthcoming from depreciation and the profit returns of the airlines if the regulatory policies and conditions of the mid-1970s were continued. Although additional cash flow could be generated by equity financing, at least one-third of the amount needed to finance $19 billion would not be available to the airlines from this source by the mid-1980s.[38] As with electricity and gas, service shortages, and queues, would then occur from insufficient flights. These shortages would be harder to detect, though, since they would appear in reservation backlogs or airport waiting lines rather than in some consumers being cut off entirely.

The prospect of insufficient flights would be real so long as CAB regulation was to continue. However, the regulatory reform plan passed by Congress and put into effect at the end of 1978 calls for a five-year transition to complete deregulation of passenger fares and airline entry into city-pair markets. In that period, minimum fares will no longer be controlled by the board, and the fare level can also increase each year by 5 percent more than inflation without formal rate case review. Given these changes, and given that cost increases can be contained because of the increased flexibility in rate setting, the expected cash flow for the airlines will be better than predicted above. The opportunity to increase fares at least partially free of regulation could allow these companies to generate the investment needed to guarantee high-quality service in the 1980s. Thus the prospects for airline service are the same as for deregulation of this industry.

The railroads have somewhat the same prospects in the coming decade, but for slightly different reasons. In the presence of rising fuel, labor, and capital costs, the Interstate Commerce Commission granted revenue increases almost every year since 1967 that kept the rail rate index in line with general price-level changes. But the commission was not flexible in allowing reductions of service on lines experiencing greater than average cost increases. The railroads thus had to continue to provide for small shippers, those on short-distance lines, and those seeking small volume but frequent service, even though unit costs for these services increased more rapidly than revenues. To meet service requirements there and still earn profits, rate-cost margins were increased on high-volume and long-distance transport.

While this distortion of their rate structures did maintain profit rates for lines with a balance of both types of traffic, it also provided incentives for the further expansion of trucking companies into the high-profit-margin services.[39] Competition from trucking and barge lines for the higher volume services took away rail traffic that was supposed to provide earnings to subsidize low-density service.

Over the coming decade, the outlook is for more of the same. Rate increases will have to be larger to maintain overall positive profits and thus provide for investment to maintain capacity. But higher rates, in turn, will accelerate the shift away from rail transport. The end result may very well be to experience reduced service quality on both high- and low-density routes as the railroads lose the capacity to serve both kinds of demand.

The shift of resources away from rail transportation has already proceeded to a considerable extent. The railroads have deferred maintenance to such an extent that, unless large-scale investments

77

are made in the early 1980s in existing plant, the profitability of most of the Eastern and Midwest companies will disappear. If such investment is not made, operating costs will rise and the quality of service is likely to deteriorate to such an extent that demands for service will be reduced by a large percentage. With higher costs and lower demands, regulated rate increases would be ineffective in preventing further reductions in service quality. The end of those adjustments would be a greatly reduced rail system, with or without a shortage of service.

These discouraging prospects can of course be improved by changes in regulation just as they can with the airlines. The ICC's rulings on abandonments and on rate levels can determine whether this pattern of behavior prevails. If abandonment of low-density routes is accelerated and if rate levels increase immediately with new investment—in effect, if deregulation takes place—then maintenance and replacement of capacity on high-density routes could still be accomplished.

The national telephone system is probably going to be last in line to experience the dampening effects of regulation under inflation. To be sure, the telephone industry has already seen some of these changes, but not of the magnitude to affect overall earnings, investment, and provisions of service. During the mid-1960s a regulatory pattern was established in which increases in monthly residential charges were kept below increases in the costs of providing local service, while rate increases on long-distance toll services were greater than their cost increases. With rising input costs during the later inflationary period, this pattern of rate distortion continued. Toll rates and service charges were increased by the FCC and the state regulatory agencies, but in a way that reduced further the rate-cost margin on residential and other local services. Most of the margin increases occurred on long-distance services, where rates were allowed to increase slightly each year while costs were still decreasing due to substantial economies of new technology and of scale. By the middle 1970s, local access and usage charges were two-thirds the marginal costs of providing these services, while long-distance rates were two times the marginal costs of those services.[40] Such high profit margins on toll services fostered entry by specialized telecommunications companies into the long-distance business service markets—entry allowed by the FCC in the late 1960s and early 1970s with new certification of new specialized systems. But at the same time no new revenue sources for subsidizing local service were found by the state regulatory commissions, even though the established national companies were expected to continue to expand local service.

The long-run outlook under regulation for these regulated full-service telephone companies has to be similar to that of the other public-utility and transportation companies. Profitability will be reduced in high-margin markets as traffic is diverted. But profitability will not be allowed to increase in low-margin markets, given that the commissions disallow rate increases on basic service. The companies will experience an overall decline in profitability, which has to lead to reduced investment and ultimately reduced service. This may take a number of years if the operating companies continue to keep cost increases down. Even so, stringency in allowing selective rate increases in the presence of inflation can be expected to reduce service in the telecommunications field just as it has in the regulated energy and transportation industries.

Resistance by the regulatory agencies in the 1970s to price increases was widespread and effective, whether in holding down the across-the-board increases proposed in natural gas and electricity, or the selective adjustments necessary to end cross-subsidies in railroad and telephone services. Regulation reduced profitability in some industries to levels below those required to sustain the quality and growth of service. That is, low regulated profit rates reduced the rate of growth of investment, and sooner or later investment curtailment reduced growth in the production of regulated goods and services. The outlook under regulation is for more such service deterioration—a condition that is critical but not urgent, given the slow and indirect way in which present price controls are transformed into future production shortages. Of course this outlook might improve, if inflation abates and if regulation is reformed. But that is the subject of the last chapter.

3

◇◇◇◇◇

Health and
Safety Regulation

As the impact of overregulation was beginning to be felt by the public utilities and the transportation and communications industries in the late 1960s, other industries were broadly undertaking an experiment with a new type of regulation. Beginning in the mid-1960s Congress enacted legislation establishing agencies to administer standards for industrial health and safety, for consumer product safety, and for maintaining the quality of the environment. The reasons for such additional regulation were many and diverse. But fundamental to government action in these areas was the awakening of public awareness that action was necessary. Such well-publicized portents of disaster as Rachel Carson's *Silent Spring* and Ralph Nader's *Unsafe at Any Speed*[1] were certainly significant influences, both on public opinion and government action. The general view that there were social problems created by industrial production that were not being dealt with was confirmed by reports of higher death rates due to smog and industrial accidents. Furthermore, this heightened public awareness came at a time when new federal government programs were looked upon as the preferred way to solve problems in the Great Society.

There were two major reasons why Congress and the state legislatures turned to new regulatory agencies rather than to other types of governmental programs to make production and consumption safer and cleaner. For one, the agencies were attractive as new government activities because their costs were imposed on producers and consumers rather than being carried in the national budget. For another, there was at that time rather widespread approval of the use of the regulatory process to reduce exposure to unacceptable market behavior. The consensus view was that agency controls worked well; that, for example, the public utilities and the transportation companies had been held in bounds quite successfully by the regulatory agencies. To be sure, there were new indications that price regulation was not working very well, but these findings appeared only in the professional journals in law, political science, and economics. Regulation generally received high grades because the agencies completed their dockets of case reviews, protests against their decisions were few, and the results of it all were reliable service at stable prices.

The new regulation began with congressional legislation stating the need to protect health, safety, and the environment; setting goals for improvements in the present condition; and establishing the commissions to deal with the day-to-day problems of actually achieving the goals. Once established, the new agencies attempted to settle quickly into full-blown and efficient administrative processes. Congress was not much assistance on that endeavor. While the legislation provided guidelines as to why the new agency should proceed, it usually did not specify the method or process of regulation.

In fact the various approaches taken in early regulatory decisions came down to using well-known processes of licensing company operations. The agencies learned from prior operations in regulating drug safety or retailer fraud. From these examples came the open case docket and the adversary process at the hearing on health or safety conditions. With the use of trial-like practices, emphasis was placed on data and case materials on physical conditions of production and distribution associated with plant, equipment, operating mode, or actual transaction.

By the middle 1970s, this regulation was deciding cases on standards some distance from the goals laid out by Congress during the Great Society ten years earlier. While legislation specified societal performance, regulatory decisions were based on operating plant or equipment conditions only indirectly related to the occurrence of health and safety throughout the community. How far in this direction regulation went is the subject of the remaining sections of this chapter. Three important agencies are taken as representative of processes and results, the Environmental Protection Agency (EPA), the National Highway Traffic Safety Administration (NHTSA), and the Occupational Safety and Health Administration (OSHA).

The Processes of Social Regulation in Detail

Once installed in the Executive Office by Congress, EPA, NHTSA, and OSHA developed their own institutions and practices. These were necessarily based at first on strict statute interpretation of goals, which more often than not led to an ever-increasing work load. They were gradually modified to adopt less direct methods that worked in reducing the load. In this way, case procedures became quite similar and began to depend on the same kind of information that determined decisions. The results can be demonstrated by examining the specific experiences of these three agencies in turn.

Although there had been local nuisance laws pertaining to pollution for decades in the 1960s, the federal government set new pollution policy by establishing regional programs for air-pollution abatement in the Clean Air Act of 1963 (Public Law 88-206 of that year) and the Air Quality Act of 1967 (Public Law 90-148). The second of these two acts provided for the establishment of air-quality standards and for federal agency limits on emissions of motor vehicles "As soon as practicable, given appropriate consideration to technological feasibility and economic costs." The

Clean Air Act Amendments of 1970 (Public Law 91-604) were passed by Congress to "speed up, expand, and intensify the war against air pollution in the United States with a view to assuring that the air we breathe throughout the nation is wholesome once again." To achieve these goals federal regulatory authorities were to establish national air-quality standards. In 1971 standards went into effect for five major criteria pollutants: sulfur oxides, particulates, carbon monoxide, hydrocarbons, and photochemical oxidants.

In addition, for the first time, Congress set specific product performance standards by stating the maximum allowed emissions of hydrocarbons, carbon monoxide, and other pollutants from automobiles. Deadlines for meeting these standards were extended in the Clean Air Act Amendments of 1977 (Public Law 95-95) and the process itself was extended with provisions in Section 109 (H) which permitted the EPA administrator to use design standards rather than performance standards: "If in the judgment of the administrator it is not feasible to prescribe or enforce a standard of performance he may instead promulgate a design, equipment, work practice or operational standard or combination thereof which reflects the best technological system of continuous emission reduction" (91 STAT. 699).

The Environmental Protection Agency was organized as a branch of the Executive Office in 1971, bringing together the various air and water quality and safety offices of other departments. In its day-to-day operations to regulate both air and water quality, EPA turned to setting limits on pollution emitted by a plant or vehicle per unit of operation—what might be termed product performance standards—even though the Clean Air Act was framed in terms of goals for regional air, water, and land quality. Moreover, the product performance standards were usually formulated with particular pollution-control methods in mind so that they in effect implied equipment design standards. The standards were mostly the same across plants so that they were insensitive to differences in water or air quality resulting from different combinations of emissions or meteorological conditions at any one location.

While standards were uniform and equipment specific, their application varied widely in the operations of the different state environmental-control agencies. Postponements and waivers were granted, based on economic hardship to the company or community, or on the ability of the agency to handle only a limited number of cases. Exceptions were most frequently found where results from enforcement would be most substantial. Whatever the reasons, numerous exceptions and variances in issuing permits rendered the uniform standards process less than completely effective.

The evolving methods and practices of automobile safety regulation also transformed general performance into specific equipment standards. The public policy of highway safety began with the establishment of two agencies in the Department of Commerce in 1966, the National Traffic Safety Agency (under Public Law 89-563) and the National Highway Safety Agency (under Public Law 89-564). These agencies were combined by executive order in 1967 to form the National Highway Safety Bureau in the new Department of Transportation. In 1970 the bureau was reorganized as the National Highway Traffic Safety Administration (NHTSA). The purpose of regulation in the 1966 act was "to reduce traffic accidents and deaths and injuries to persons resulting from traffic accidents. . . . [by] establish[ing] motor vehicle safety standards for motor vehicles and equipment in interstate commerce and . . . undertake [ing to] support necessary safety research and development." As indicated in the Senate Report on the Motor Vehicle Safety Act of 1966, the overriding consideration in the issuance of standards was the reduction of accidents and mortality on the highway.[2]

This performance mandate was supplemented by Section 102 (2) of Public Law 89-563 which defined the necessary safety standards as "the minimum standard for motor vehicle performance, or motor vehicle equipment performance, whichever is practicable, meets the need for motor vehicle safety, and provides objective criteria.'' In its operations over the years, while justifying decisions on the basis of accident-reduction goals, NHTSA set standards which amounted in practice to specifying equipment for most of the important components of automobiles. This occurred because, in order to establish operations quickly, the two original agencies adopted the Government Services Administration equipment standards for government-purchased vehicles and those of the Society of Automotive Engineers for vehicle safety. Both of these sets of standards were design-oriented, as were later NHTSA regulations related to accident avoidance, crash-injury reduction, and postcrash protection. As these standards were filled out it become clear that accident reductions were to be achieved by means of extremely detailed vehicle performance specifications which in turn could be achieved only by a few variants on certain pieces of equipment.[3]

The regulation of worker safety went even further toward specifying equipment. The Occupational Safety and Health Act of 1970 was enacted to reverse the rising trend of worker accidents during the 1960s. When the act became law in 1971, the secretary of labor set the first safety standards based on equipment specifications arrived at over the previous two decades by industry health associations and nonprofit safety organizations. They contained extremely detailed specifications of the physical conditions of production, ranging from the cleanliness of the working area to the position and size of mesh screens over moving machinery. For example, wooden ladder safety standards provided that ''the general slope of grain shall not be steeper than 1 in 15 rungs and cleats. For all ladders cross-grain not steeper than 1 in 12 are permitted.''[4] In the end, the OSHA safety ''consensus'' standards were the most detailed equipment rules extant.

By 1973 the standards most frequently violated were in machine guarding, electrical codes, placement and condition of fire extinguishers, floor and wall openings, walking and working surfaces, and in flammable or combustible liquids.[5] These were also the categories of standards developed in the greatest detail and, because of the detail, most often applied by OSHA inspection officers. There were fewer violations in other parts of the production process because plant activities there had not been covered by standards. New standards in these areas had not been written and proposed by the late 1970s because of the prolonged, litigious process required for adoption of changes or additions to the original consensus standards. The resulting unevenness in safety regulation in American industry corresponds to the variance in enforcement of EPA pollution control.

Thus there has evolved a system for applying this new regulation. Although goals were set in terms of improving health and safety across the country, EPA, NHTSA, and OSHA regulations evolved away from performance to setting out and partially enforcing detailed equipment specifications. Because standard setting has been litigious and prolonged, the existing set of rules has not been complete. But these regulations when available and applied to the individual plant have proven to be extremely detailed and inflexible. When they have not fit, the only way to resolve an all-or-nothing confrontation has been to postpone application.

Given such a system the problems in operating under the statute may have been enough to negate the intended results. This is to be determined by measuring as completely as possible the costs and benefits of health and safety regulation.

The Cost Effects of EPA, NHTSA, and OSHA Regulations

By controlling equipment and production processes, the agencies regulating health and safety should have had some impact on industry costs and prices. The impact would have been realized by the companies in higher equipment costs and reduced equipment options. This, in turn, would have increased the long-run, and might have increased the short-run, costs of production. In time, higher costs result in price increases. Whether the price impact was significant during the early 1970s, the initial years of social regulation, is the question here.

In fact, there were substantial additional investments made to deal with the requirements of EPA, OSHA, and NHTSA in equipment specifications. Purchases of plant and equipment required by regulations were concentrated in a few industries, however. Pollution-related investment for 1975 was $6.6 billion. Five industries—electric utilities, petroleum refining, chemicals, nonferrous metals, and paper—accounted for 70 percent of these expenditures.[6] More important, these mandated expenditures accounted for a large share of the total investment outlays in these industries. For these five and also for the construction materials and steel industries, more than 10 percent of total net investment was devoted to pollution abatement. For safety-related regulations in conjunction with NHTSA equipment requirements the automobile companies extended their outlays by more than $0.5 billion.[7] As a result of OSHA regulations, companies throughout the economy spent $4 billion that year for equipment to increase safety in the workplace.[8] Again, certain industries bore most of these expenses— the chemical, metals, wood, paper, and automobile industries.

With such expenditures on safety and pollution reductions, companies in the industries most subject to the new controls must have experienced some increases in production costs. Even in the short run, the cost increases from operating the new equipment would have resulted in higher prices and thereby in reduced output growth. In the long run, diversion of investment to satisfy regulatory requirements should have led to lower growth of capacity and consequently to higher prices and less production once again.

Indeed, the price increases in those industries most impacted by new investment requirements were greater during the early years of health and safety regulation than in those industries not yet subject to regulation. The exceptions were the electric utilities and the petroleum-refining industry, which were price-regulated through all or part of the period. Otherwise the seven most regulated industries had average annual price changes for 1973–77 which were greater than or equal to those elsewhere during the same period and also higher than those in the same industries for the preceding three years (see Table 3.1). Specifically, during 1969–73, prices in these industries increased by 1.7 percent more than in other industries and during 1973–77 prices increased by 1.6 percent more than elsewhere.[9] This high rate of price increase cannot be attributed solely to rapid economy-wide inflation, given that production in these most regulated industries grew at lower annual rates than in other industries (see Table 3.1). With only one exception, that of the chemicals industry, their production decreases were greater than the average rate of decline for less regulated industries during the 1973–77 period. Even though some of these cutbacks were probably associated with the 1974–75 cyclical downturn, particularly in materials and construction, the magnitudes were so great that they must have been at last partially the result of the rising costs associated with regulation, which in turn caused larger price increases and lower demand growth than elsewhere in the economy.

This industry reaction to regulation is indicated particularly by the behavior of the most regulated industries during this period as compared with their behavior during similar earlier cycles when they were not regulated. Table 3.2 shows that 1973–75 industry price changes[10] mostly matched or exceeded earlier price increases. Output changes in 1973–75 diverged sharply from earlier periods, sustaining substantial declines. Furthermore, in earlier periods of high inflation and GNP growth, those previously unregulated industries had had a tendency to lead in production gains when compared with all industries. The fact that, during the 1973–75 inflation, price increases and output reductions in these industries were greater than in earlier periods or in other industries confirms the existence of a price-increasing impact from the new regulations.

Did this price impact encompass most of the new costs of regulation? If so, consumers in effect paid for the equipment outlays

TABLE 3.1 *Price and Production Changes in Those Industries Subject to Health and Safety Regulation*

Industry	Price changes		Production changes	
	1969–73	1973–77	1969–73	1973–77
	(average annual rate of change in percent)			
Automobiles	0.9[a]	14.2[a]	2.3[b]	−3.8[b]
Mining	9.3	8.7	1.4	−1.8
Construction	10.2	7.4	−1.2	−0.6
Paper	1.8	10.6	5.6	−1.3
Chemicals	1.2	9.0	5.2	2.4
Stone, clay, and glass	4.4	8.3	3.5	−0.5
Primary metals	4.5	13.8	2.0	−5.1
Other manufacturing	2.8	7.9	2.7	0.6

[a]The measure of automobile price change here is the Consumer Price Index as compiled by the U.S. Department of Labor.

[b]The measure of automobile production change is retail sales in units as compiled by the U.S. Department of Commerce.

SOURCE: U.S. Department of Commerce, *Workfile 1205-02-02*, 1978 revision.

TABLE 3.2 *Comparative Performance during Inflationary Periods of Industries Subject to Health and Safety Regulation*

Industry	1947–48		1950–51		1973–75	
	Prices	Output	Prices	Output	Prices	Output
			(average annual rates of change in percent)			
Automobiles	7.6	8.4	−0.3	−4.8	6.4	−14.1
Mining	16.3	6.4	3.8	8.5	13.3	−6.9
Construction	9.2	15.7	6.4	11.4	10.6	−7.4
Paper	14.9	−8.7	17.8	6.9	21.0	−13.1
Chemicals	−3.7	26.4	12.6	6.8	15.5	−6.5
Stone, clay, and glass	8.3	7.9	5.9	7.5	10.8	−10.7
Primary metals	11.7	1.9	6.3	20.6	20.5	−10.0
Other manufacturing	6.9	4.7	12.5	5.4	10.8	−5.7

SOURCE: See Table 3.1.

required by health and safety regulations. An indication as to whether this happened is found in profit margins and rates of return in the most regulated industries. If these were maintained despite the new regulations then the effects were passed on in price increases. In fact, profit margins on sales in these industries declined very slightly (by 2 to 3 percentage points during 1970–73 as compared with the previous period), while margins for unregulated manufacturing companies fell by little more than one percentage point (see Table 3.3). This slight margin decline did not substantially reduce returns to investors in most of the regulated industries. Average annual investors' rates of return were low in the automobile, primary metals, and chemicals industries in the late 1960s, but returns were high in the other four heavily regulated industries in this period. Only the automobile, glass, and metals industries had returns below comparable investments in the early 1970s. These comparisons of profitability over business cycles and with less regulated industries suggest that most of these regulatory cost increases were passed on to consumers.

Another cost, however, consists of the opportunity losses from the long-run reduction in goods and services resulting from reduced investments and growth. As prices rise and demand is reduced in the regulated industries, production or investment there is replaced by that in the pollution-control- and occupational-safety-equipment industries. Total GNP should thus be the same with or without controls, given that monetary and fiscal policy eliminate any unemployment involved in transferring resources to the new control-equipment industries. But there would still be some long-run substitution of control equipment for capital investment, so as to reduce the growth of GNP generated from capital. To the extent that this occurs, full-capacity GNP would increase at a lower rate. Although such results from regulation have probably not been substantial, GNP growth could be reduced in the early 1980s by up to .5 percent per annum if the announced pollution-abatement goals for the mid-1980s were to be met.[11] Even if they were not put into effect, the continuation of present

TABLE 3.3 *Rates of Return in Industries Subject to Social Regulation*

Industry	Profit margins on sales (percent)		Return on investors' value (difference of actual from expected returns) (percent)	
	1966–69	1970–73	1966–69	1970–73
Automobiles	15.2	11.6	−0.9 (−5.7)[a]	1.5 (−2.2)
Mining	19.7	17.4	7.7 (+2.8)	6.4 (+2.2)
Construction	9.2	6.7	13.3 (+8.4)	13.6 (+9.6)
Paper	13.6	10.3	6.0 (+1.0)	5.2 (+0.9)
Chemicals	16.6	14.8	−1.2 (−6.1)	9.0 (+4.8)
Stone, clay, and glass	15.6	12.7	5.9 (+0.9)	−2.3 (−6.6)
Primary metals	13.7	8.6	1.1 (−4.0)	2.5 (−2.2)
Unregulated manufacturing	14.1	12.7	7.5 (+2.6)	4.5 (+0.4)
Market return			5.0	4.3

[a] See notes *a* and *b* in Table 2.6.

SOURCE: See Standard & Poor's Corporation, *Compustat*, September 1978 revision.

trends in regulation would result in such capacity growth reductions that the level of GNP could be 3 to 5 percent lower by the mid-1980s.[12]

In sum, there are two costs of regulation observable in the economic activity of firms subject to the new regulation in the early 1970s. The companies in those industries most subject to health and safety controls went through a period of more rapid acceleration of prices and greater reductions of output growth. In effect, consumers paid for regulation in higher prices. The investment pattern resulting from regulation, in which capital outlays were shifted to purchasing pollution-abatement and occupational-safety equipment, did not greatly affect current employment and production levels. In the future, however, it could reduce somewhat the trend rate of growth of the economy. Then the consumer would pay once again, by doing without goods and services that otherwise would be available if controls had not been put into effect.

These reductions, however, might be more than compensated for by a higher quality of life, given less pollution and fewer industrial and highway accidents. These gains even though not accounted for in dollar gross national product could be so substantial as to be worth the goods and services forgone as a result of the regulatory requirements.

The Benefits from Environmental and Safety Regulation

The reductions in pollution and in accident and illness rates due to the initiation of regulation by OSHA, NHTSA, and EPA should be observable. However, analysts have been unable to find significant reductions in the unhealthful conditions which were to be dealt with by the new regulatory activities.

Research on OSHA regulation has indicated that there have not been significant and widespread reductions in worker accident rates from agency activities. Perhaps not much could have been expected, given that OSHA's activities have been narrowly lim-

The ⁂ Presidents Association

October 1979

Dear PA Member:

Government regulation of business has become a great
confusion that ultimately benefits no one. With a
highly inefficient cost-benefit ratio, growing regulation has saddled business with burgeoning overhead
and limited growth horizons, and has given the public
rising prices and poorer quality goods and services.

It's a complex history that led to this sorry state,
but one that The Regulated Industries traces with
evenhanded clarity and full documentation. Sizing up
the current scene, author Paul W. MacAvoy of the Yale
University School of Organization and Management
states that regulations "have spread to encompass
rather completely those industries responsible for
about one-fifth of GNP and have had the effect of reducing economy-wide production as a result. There
apparently have been no commensurate social benefits
from this regulatory activity." Full reform is the
only solution, says Professor MacAvoy, who has served
on the Council of Economic Advisers, but he believes
the prospects for this are "bleak."

This is not a book you will enjoy, but in its necessary and clear definition of the problem, it is a
book I believe you will appreciate.

Sincerely,

Ronald P. Myers

Ronald P. Myers
Executive Vice President
and General Manager

The Presidents Association

October 1979

Dear PA Member:

Government regulation of business has become a great
confusion that ultimately benefits no one. With a
highly inefficient cost-benefit ratio, growing regulation has saddled business with burgeoning overhead
and limited growth horizons, and has given the public
rising prices and poorer quality goods and services.

It's a complex history that led to this sorry state,
but one that The Regulated Industries traces with
evenhanded clarity and full documentation. Sizing up
the current scene, author Paul W. MacAvoy of the Yale
University School of Organization and Management
states that regulations "have spread to encompass
rather completely those industries responsible for
about one-fifth of GNP and have had the effect of reducing economy-wide production as a result. There
apparently have been no commensurate social benefits
from this regulatory activity." Full reform is the
only solution, says Professor MacAvoy, who has served
on the Council of Economic Advisers, but he believes
the prospects for this are "bleak."

This is not a book you will enjoy, but in its necessary and clear definition of the problem, it is a
book I believe you will appreciate.

Sincerely,

Ronald P. Myers
Executive Vice President
and General Manager

ited to regulating plant and equipment specifications when worker training, supervision, incentives, and plant routine all play an important role in accident prevention as well. OSHA as an administrative agency became concerned with equipment when work flow and employee activity rates probably had more to do with rising accident rates in the late 1960s. Even so, that there have been no discernible effects at all from regulation is surprising.

In a study of the impact of the state agencies enforcing OSHA equipment standards, Paul E. Sands found that these regulatory activities had little observable impact on injury rates, whether there was relatively more or less enforcement.[13] This might have been a result of the generally low level of state operations (with state agencies spending no more than one dollar per year per worker on supervision and enforcement of the control program). But OSHA's national efforts in the early 1970s to reduce accident levels in particular industries, both by stepping up enforcement across industries generally and by shifting substantial surveillance and enforcement resources to these industries, had no more of an effect on accident rates. According to Robert Smith, vigorous enforcement of OSHA standards did not reduce factory accidents in the cases where extensive additional resources were put into enforcement. Also, research by Aldona DiPietro, based on comparisons between companies that had and had not been inspected, showed that OSHA inspection made no difference in accident rates. In fact, in more than half the cases, higher accident rates were associated with more inspection activities by the agency.[14]

These studies all evaluated OSHA's operations. A more definitive analysis of the results from regulation provides an assessment of the presence versus the absence of controls. In a detailed study of the California experience with OSHA-type regulation, John Mendeloff found that the lost-workday injury rate was not significantly reduced after regulation began in that state. The study also attempted to measure OSHA-like impacts by focusing on several specific types of injuries identified by safety engineers as most likely to be affected by OSHA's design-standard regulatory process. Concentrating on a comparison of experience before and after OSHA began operations, Mendeloff used data from the pre-OSHA period to predict the lost-workday injury rate in manufacturing industries if OSHA had not existed. The actual post-OSHA lost-workday rates were in fact smaller than those predicted for OSHA-free operations. This suggests that OSHA did reduce accident rates, but the difference between the predicted and actual rates was insignificant.[15]

In all, OSHA did not establish a pattern of widespread or effective work-condition regulation, and thus there was no substantial impact on accident rates consequent from this type of regulation in the 1970s. But even though these poor results may have been the product of sporadic inspection and enforcement, there should have been improvements over time: "Firms normally come into compliance when they replace obsolete machinery. . . . manufacturers are unlikely to offer equipment that violates standards [and] in fact in one case the manufacturers of mechanical power presses supported a tougher standard on the assumption that many more firms buy new machines rather than modify old ones under tougher standards."[16] That there were not significant improvements was due in part to gaps in enforcement, but more fundamentally due to the fact that equipment controls did not center on accident reduction.

NHTSA regulation of automobiles produced somewhat the same results. In the early years of operation, the two highway safety agencies directed their regulatory activities toward improving crash survivability. They issued twenty-nine motor-vehicle equipment standards and proposed ninety-five more during 1967 and 1968. These recommendations included requiring cars to be equipped with "passive occupant restraint systems" such as inflatable air bags which increased survivability in crashes for front-seat occupants. In subsequent years, the NHTSA agencies implemented rules on "impact protection for the driver from the steering control system," on seating systems, seat-belt installation and assembly, seat-belt assembly anchorages, child seating systems, the flammability of interior materials, and the strength of side doors, windows, and bumpers. The NHTSA view was that the "reductions in the number of casualties per crash can be substantially attributed to this emphasis." The goal to be achieved by these regulations was to decrease the fatality rate per 100 million vehicle-miles by one-third—from 5.4 in 1968 to 3.6 in 1980. The agency stated that "the goal of reducing accident fatalities and injuries is feasible if sufficient resources are devoted on a priority basis to activities which assure a high payoff in loss reduction."[17]

By 1975 the annual NHTSA report indicated the difference between these goals and actual operations under regulation. The agency acknowledged that "many of the first safety standards were based on the Society of Automotive Engineer standards already subscribed to by much of the automotive industry. . . . [but] since [then regulation has] developed standards in advance of industry but within the state of the art, such as those on passive restraints." This was to indicate that in its first few years the agency had been promulgating existing safety criteria, so no significant results could be expected. The agency also acknowledged that "the first standards tended to specify the type of the design, such as the type of glazing to be used in windows. . . . To allow manufacturers more flexibility and opportunity for innovation, standards now state performance specifications which manufacturers must meet." Thus the original standards had been design standards. Attempts were made later to move away from design to performance standards, but it was not altogether clear, even by the time of the 1975 *Annual Report,* whether this had been achieved to any significant extent.

Whatever the type of standards, NHTSA considered itself responsible for substantial reductions in traffic fatality rates. The agency stated in 1975 that "the traffic fatality rate has gone down 35.3% since inauguration of the National Traffic Safety Drive in 1967, and 16% since 1973. . . . Though assessment of benefits is not possible program-by-program, the cumulative effect of the combination of programs is undeniable." But the reduction in

1974 accident levels was widely acknowledged to be the result of the establishment of the 55 MPH national speed limit. As NHTSA itself indicated, "While the country experienced reductions in overall highway travel in 1974 of approximately 2.6%, the reduction in the number of total accidents was about 5% and [in] the number of fatalities was about 17%. . . . [these being] safety benefits derived from the establishment of the 55 MPH limit."[18] These benefits were due to energy conservation policies following from the OPEC oil embargo and the ensuing energy crisis of that year. Thus recent highway accident rates have been lower in part because of energy policy, not safety regulation.

The regulation-improved automobile could still be credited with some part of the change in accident rates. The consideration in giving such credit is with whether the trend toward reduced casualties observed after NHTSA began operations was or was not established before NHTSA or its predecessors had been conceived. Specifically, the question is whether the important determinants of increased highway safety were regulatory or other factors. For the preregulation period, accidents per vehicle-mile were explained by (1) the cost of accident insurance, (2) personal income levels, (3) driving speed, (4) driver age, (5) alcoholic intoxication, and (6) a secular trend.[19] When the statistical equation for this relation for the preregulation period was used to generate predictions of accidents for the period after mandatory safety devices were introduced, it was found that projected highway fatality rates without regulation differed very little from actual rates under regulation.

This discrediting of regulation is surprising given the observed decline in fatality rates in the late 1960s under regulation. But the low rate without regulation after 1966 "can be explained directly by non-regulatory forces, the most important of which is demographic."[20] The peaking of the birth rate around 1950 led to slower growth of the population of driving age under twenty-five during the late 1960s. With fewer young drivers, there were fewer fatal accidents. And at the same time, drivers acted responsibly to reduce accident rates without special regard to the required safety equipment because accidents cost them more, driving conditions were better, and they had more economically at stake in an accident.

To be sure, these findings are controversial. This economic analysis by Professor Peltzman of accident rates does not take account of all the causal factors, such as adoption of more light-weight automobiles which makes driving less safe, or changes in highway construction and maintenance. Fitting of a somewhat different equation resulted in indications that fatality rates were reduced by regulation after 1965.[21] On the whole, however, the predominant effects of population and trend cast substantial doubt on the assertion that early NHTSA regulations were effective in reducing accident fatalities.

Further investigations along these lines were undertaken in 1976 by the General Accounting Office.[22] The GAO analysts compared injury and death rates across model years in a sample of more than two million automobiles involved in accidents, and found that from 15 to 25 percent fewer deaths and serious injuries to drivers occurred in the 1966–68 model year automobiles first subject to safety regulation. This was not necessarily contradictory to the earlier Peltzman findings of "no effect," because it did not account for the effect of safer vehicles on accident rates and thus on automobile nondriver occupant and pedestrian fatalities. This study also indicated that there were not further reductions in driver death and injury rates in later model years due to more extensive regulation. In this and previous studies, the important variables determining mortality rates were alcoholic intoxication, the weight of the car, the type of accident, the type of road, and, last of all, the model year associated with equipment characteristics. Thus the major studies of NHTSA together perhaps indicate some initial impact from regulatory operations on driver but not pedestrian safety. NHTSA cannot be said to have been widely effective in the direction and to the extent required in its mandate to bring safety to the highways.

The benefits of EPA regulation have not been more important

than those in the other two agencies. Although positive effects of environmental controls have appeared at certain locations, on the whole they have not been significant or widespread. Where the EPA or the state environmental agencies have invoked rules against pollution by a company at a specific location, there usually has been a reduction of emissions at that point. Certain rivers and air corridors have been made cleaner than they were five years ago because of such actions. However, since standards for each industry have been developed and enforced to some degree for a number of years, it could be expected that regulation would have greatly improved nationwide air and water quality. This has not been the case.

There were numerous examples of important results in the middle 1970s. In its 1977 *Annual Report,* the Council on Environmental Quality (CEQ) reported, "from 1967 to 1976 hydrocarbon emissions in the San Francisco area were reduced 25 percent and daily observed oxidant levels also declined 25 percent." There was also significant improvement in carbon monoxide pollution in New York City: "Although New York's carbon monoxide problem is still severe, projections based on correlated data show greater improvement than anticipated." The report on Los Angeles was not as encouraging: "Its special geography, climate and dependence on cars may prevent Los Angeles from achieving the oxidant standard."[23]

Significant improvements also were made in the middle 1970s in the quality of some waterways—as measured by reduced waste loads and bacterial content. The CEQ stated that, based on detailed and comprehensive monitoring of twelve rivers across the country, five rivers showed "significant overall improvement in fecal coliform violation rates: The Willamette, the Colorado, the Red River, the Ohio and the Tennessee Rivers." In particular, "water quality in the Willamette has dramatically improved during the previous decade and even though it has continued sanitary problems they are mostly related to runoff sewer overflows during high flow periods." This progress is taken as indicative of positive results from regulating community and company emissions and discharges.[24]

The gains that have been made in air and water quality on a national scale have been quite limited, however, as has been acknowledged by these agencies. Both EPA and CEQ found compliance with regulatory standards in only about one-third of the nation's air-quality regions. Total emissions were reduced substantially in the early 1970s for only two of the six major air pollutants—particulates, and carbon monoxide—and slightly for two more—hydrocarbons and sulfur dioxide. Emissions of nitrogen oxides increased in this period, although at a slower rate than in previous periods.[25]

Even these limited gains probably did not result alone from enforcement of national environmental standards. Many industry-specific standards were put in place after product and process improvements already underway were beginning to reduce pollution. Pollutants were being reduced because it was profitable, given new technology, to conserve products that had been previously discharged as waste. Automobile emissions of the major pollutants were being reduced by improvements in fuel-burning performance in new models each year, for example. Regulation of auto emissions may have done little beyond taking credit for the improvements that would have been saleable in any event. In this context, the new regulatory standards in some cases provided no more than time-period targets over which to accelerate the adoption of improvements already underway.

More likely, recent air- and water-quality changes had as much to do with cycles in industrial activity as with regulation. Emissions have been determined by levels of production in each industry. These, in turn, have been determined by economy-wide demand conditions. At least part of the gains in pollution reduction in the middle 1970s, attributed by CEQ to regulation, was probably the result of the downturns in economy-wide industrial goods production during the 1974–75 recession.

The limited role of regulation can be shown by accounting for the separate but concurrent effects on pollution load of changing technology, economic activity, and the new EPA standards. Pollutants can be measured by tonnage of emissions divided by industry GNP levels; cyclical conditions can be indicated by industry rates of capacity utilization; and changes in technology can be indicated by a time trend. The effects of the presence of regulatory standards can be measured by a binary variable. Fitting equations to estimates of values of these variables by industry with 1968–76 annual observations reveals that regulation had a significant effect in reducing pollution volume only from the automobile and electric-utility industries (see Table 3.4). In the three other industries, pollution-reduction trends already present before regulation were the major cause of improvements. But evaluating all industries and regulations together, the combined equation for 1968–76 showed that trend significantly reduced pollutant load and regulation insignificantly increased the pollutant load. The general finding has to be that the new pollution-control regulations did not change the pollution load on the economy.

On the whole, although EPA, NHTSA, and OSHA themselves have made estimates from time to time indicating improved conditions, there had been no significant improvement from national equipment standards through the middle 1970s. There may be better results forthcoming after these agencies have been in operation for a greater length of time. But there may not be, since policies and practices now fully established and in place are having the intended effect and are not likely to produce different kinds of effects in the future.

It is clear that the health and safety regulatory system has increased prices and reduced GNP in the most regulated industries. These conditions have probably been realized to an important extent already. There have been indications that, because of drawing attention toward equipment and away from behavior, the control system had also not brought about improvements generally in health, safety, and environmental quality as of the late 1970s. In other words, these regulatory agencies have been having a sub-

TABLE 3.4 Regulatory Effects on Pollution

Sector	Trend effects on pollution volume[a]	Cycle effects on pollution volume[a]	Regulatory effects on pollution volume[a]	Percentage of the variation in pollution explained by these factors (R^2)
Minerals production	Positive	Positive	Negative	.61
Automobile utilization	Positive	n.a.	*Negative*	.98
Chemical production	Negative	Negative	Positive	.62
Primary metals	*Negative*	Negative	Positive	.76
Electric utilities	Negative	Positive	*Negative*	.98
Petro refining	*Negative*	Positive	Negative	.79
All industries[b]	*Negative*	Positive	Positive	.19

[a] Those coefficients statistically significant from zero are italicized where significance is according to students' t at probability of 0.05.

[b] Includes industrial, residential, commercial, and institutional fuel combustion, and oil and gas production and marketing, in addition to sectors listed.

SOURCE: Regression analysis by the author. The general form of the equations was as follows:

EMISSIONS/OUTPUT $= a_0 + a_1$ TREND $+ a_2$ CYCLE $+ a_3$ REGULATION $+ (a_i P_i)$, where

EMISSIONS = tons of pollutant i (EPA, unpublished data)

OUTPUT = index of production for industry (Federal Reserve Board), except demand for gasoline (Department of Commerce)

TREND = time trend, 1968 = 1

CYCLE = index of capacity utilization for industry (Federal Reserve Board)

REGULATION = variable equals one for the presence of *regulation* of pollutant i, and zero otherwise;

P_i = dummy variable for pollutant i for four of the five major pollutants: particulates, sulfur oxides, carbon monoxide, hydrocarbons, and nitrogen oxides. For the all-industries equation, additional dummy variables were added for each industry after the first. Estimation was two-stage least squares, correcting at the first stage for serial correlation.

stantial cost effect, but not the benefits intended in the enabling legislation. They have increased costs of production, which have increased prices to consumers, without having brought about significant improvements in the safety and cleanliness of production and consumption.

4

◇◇◇◇◇

Regulatory Reform

Since president Johnson's Great Society of the late 1960s, government regulation has had an increasingly important influence on corporate decisions, in the establishment of work conditions, the setting of prices, and the determination of the quantity and quality of goods and services. Almost all corporations now are affected by some form of regulation. The impact of price controls and health and safety regulation has grown in the last decade so that for all intents and purposes the sector of the economy that could be termed "fully regulated" has more than doubled in its share of GNP.

What have been the results? Since the mid-1960s, price and entry regulation has restricted profitability so widely that production growth has been slowed down in the energy and transportation industries. Rate increases have been less than cost increases, causing declines in capacity growth and production growth in these industries during the early 1970s. As a result most of the public-utility and common-carrier industries failed to extend service to new communities or customers at quality levels comparable to those in the 1950s and early 1960s.

The output effects of health, safety, and environmental regulation were remarkably similar to those of public-utility regulation. The new agencies substantially increased the costs of providing goods and services in those industries most affected by their decisions. Because there were no price limits imposed by this regulation, the higher costs were passed on to consumers in higher prices, thereby reducing consumption growth and ultimately reducing economy-wide GNP growth. This regulation, at the cost of higher prices, should have improved environmental, health, and safety conditions. While there were cases in which that occurred, on the whole measurable improvements in safety or in the environment did not take place as a result of the operations of the federal administrative agencies established by Congress to force such improvements.

Both types of regulation have spread to encompass rather completely those industries responsible for about one-fifth of GNP and have had the effect of reducing economy-wide production as a result. There apparently have been no commensurate social benefits from this regulatory activity. These results have not been by chance, nor have they been the design of policy-makers; rather they have followed necessarily from the regulatory process. To bring about any improvement, the process has to be changed. To begin with, a reformed system would have to allow prices of the regulated companies to respond to changes in cost and demand conditions. Regulation to improve health, safety, and environmental quality would have to be reformed so that equipment specifications were replaced by performance standards that were cost-effective and beneficial. In both types of regulation, a number of operations even when improved would probably not be beneficial, so that deregulation would be the best of the alternatives.

There is some possibility of making such changes. But the reorganization of industry required by the transformation from the present state of affairs to such new types of regulation or to deregulation would be extensive and costly to the economy. Because of these costs of change, proposing reform is an exercise in benefit-cost analysis, in which the benefits from reform include the elimination of the adverse results of the present system and the costs involve social losses from industry disruption caused by the transformation to the new state of affairs.

To assess these and balance them in a concerted effort at productive change requires first some discussion of the present extent of reform. This is to be followed by delineation of the characteristics of reform, and lastly by a discussion here of the chances that it will take place.

Current Reform of Price Regulation

Because of its now adverse economic impact on the companies affected by regulation, the regulatory process has come under great pressure for change in day-to-day case hearings, in case-decision appeals in the courts, and in legislatures. In response, there has been considerable change in administrative practice; new rule-makings have replaced or accelerated the flow of case decisions and, more important, new standards have been established for case decisions on revenue increases that have relaxed previously severe limits on the size of these increases.

The most widespread means for effecting this change has been a general relaxation of the old rate-base standards in revenue request cases. There have been two means of relaxation: (1) before the case is decided, allowing more temporary rate increases, and (2) after the case has been decided, allowing a higher rate of return.

During the last few years, state regulatory commissions have been hearing larger numbers of requests for increases. Even with the old procedures however, they have greatly reduced regulatory lag. This has been accomplished by allowing proposed higher rates to take effect before the case decision has been reached, subject to repayment of any charges found to be in excess later. Although electricity case decisions in 1977 took four months longer to resolve than in 1971, rate increases took less time to put into effect than they had in the earlier period (see Table 4.1).

TABLE 4.1 *State Electric Utility Rate Cases*

Year	Number of cases	Average time from date filed to decision (months)	Average time from date filed to new effective rates (months)
1971	59	8.75	8.71
1972	101	8.98	9.19
1973	86	10.78	10.14
1974	96	11.46	9.31
1975	118	10.86	8.78
1976	131	12.52	10.52
1977	128	12.36	8.46
1978	32	13.56	8.63

NOTE: New rates can be effective before the case decision if the agency allows them on an interim basis or subject to later repayment of any excess found by the decision.

SOURCE: Edison Electric Institute.

Not only has the time period required to increase prices been greatly reduced, but the agencies and commissions also have been allowing larger price increases than during the early 1970s. For the electricity-generating companies, commission-allowed rates of return were 1.5 percentage points higher in 1977 than in 1971 (see Table 4.2). This has not been the result of changes in the methods of calculation of cost of service for rate-making. Instead, the commissions have accepted higher estimates of historical costs which reflect not current cost increases but the very large increases in equity and interest costs that occurred in the mid-1970s. Also, changes in rate base have occurred from rapid inflation in construction costs. Thus allowed revenue increases were greater in 1977 even though the electricity generating companies had about the same changes in current costs in 1971 and 1977.

There also have been changes in the standards for deciding what is to be included in costs which have allowed more rate increase. The extent to which the new costs have been included has varied from state to state. Some commissions in recent years have permitted inclusion of expenditures on construction-work-in-progress in the rate base for rate-making purposes. A few states have allowed prepayments of expenditures on materials, such as on future gas supplies by pipeline companies. In general, while the form of the process has been maintained, these changes in practices have allowed constraints on price increases to be reduced.

Even further, one qualitative change in the regulatory process has, by itself, increased rates. While the commissions have continued to receive and examine historical cost data for those categories of expanses related to providing service, they have also begun to consider for the first time estimates of future costs. This change in decision-making goes beyond merely reducing regulatory lag and using higher historical costs for rate-making purposes. It allows a wider upward revision of prices, since quite speculative estimates of future high inflation rates can be used for decision-making.

TABLE 4.2 *Returns Allowed the Electric Utilities*

Year	Number of cases	Total sales revenue test year (billions of dollars)	Total increased sales revenue sought (billions of dollars)	Average rate of return sought (percent)	Average rate of return granted (percent)	Revenue increase allowed as percent of that amount sought (percent)
1971	59	11.3	0.9	7.61	7.44	72.7
1972	101	9.6	1.0	8.01	7.64	65.6
1973	86	11.2	1.2	7.59	7.50	74.9
1974	96	12.9	1.9	8.60	8.27	79.8
1975	118	19.9	3.6	9.08	8.60	69.6
1976	131	25.3	4.5	8.35	7.88	49.0
1977	128	26.3	3.5	9.67	9.07	55.1

SOURCE: Edison Electric Institute.

Last of all, there has been legislative change. Congress mandated decontrol of railroad rates, airline-passenger fares, and natural-gas-field prices in the late 1970s. This is mentioned last only because the improvement in industry performance brought about in the last few years by these congressional acts was very limited. The Railroad Revitalization and Regulatory Reform Act of 1976 (Public Law 94-210) specifically limited rate decontrol to those markets where one or two railroads were not "dominant"[1] in providing transportation services. The Airline Deregulation Act of 1978 (Public Law 95-504) phased out regulation of passenger fares only after five years, allowing individual carrier fare reductions of up to 50 percent per year, but it limited increases to only 5 percent per year beyond inflation on competitive routes. Natural-gas deregulation took place in a number of important industrial and utility markets through a sequence of price increases allowed by emergency shortage legislation shifting buyers faced with shortages to unregulated intrastate markets from 1974 to 1977. But changes in these markets were limited to eliminating federal regulation only for the industrial users facing shortages rather than opening up unregulated intrastate markets to interstate pipelines serving household consumers as well. The Natural Gas Policy Act of 1978 (Public Law 95-621) phased out all wellhead regulated pricing, but only after six years and on different time schedules for new, onshore, offshore, and other categories of existing and future supplies. In sum, the pattern of congressional reform has been to take very small steps in decontrol by phasing out low regulated prices over half a decade.

Deregulation in Two Agencies

The important first steps in phasing out airline-passenger fare and natural-gas-control processes had already been taken by the agencies before statute changes. Both industries had been operating under ever-more-stringent price controls and, consequently, were having difficulties in adjusting to high-level inflation. The two commissions involved, the Civil Aeronautics Board (CAB) and the Federal Power Commission (FPC), had already found their methods of regulation to be unduly restrictive of rates. Guidelines for setting costs of service were too backward-looking to permit flexible price adjustments in the face of substantial cost changes. To deal with this the agencies themselves promoted their own deregulation. In the words of the CAB Chairman John Robson, "Because of regulatory inefficiencies neither the airline investor nor the consumer has fully reaped the potential benefits of the industry's enormous past productivity gains and growth."[2] The CAB in practice departed from orthodox regulations as much as possible first by relaxing scheduling and discount fare restrictions, thereby reducing passenger-mile costs. Such deregulation from within in airline controls provided enough flexibility in rates to experiment with the decontrol process and establish that service disruption did not result from the movement to open-market prices.

Natural-gas regulation had been much more restrictive than airline regulation and, as a consequence, gas markets had a greater distance to go to achieve market equilibrium. Gas shortages in the early 1970s were already as great as 20 percent of total demands. Gas market conditions were impacted by oil price increases which increased gas demand, and thus shortages, even further in the mid-1970s. Unregulated intrastate prices rose as demand increased causing gas to shift to this sector of the industry (see Table 4.3).

Deregulation to achieve an end to the shortages under these conditions was extremely complicated. The price increases required to clear interstate markets were estimated to exceed fifty cents per thousand cubic feet (MCF) in the early 1970s. On a trillion cubic feet of new interstate supplies, this would have increased consumer expenditures by $0.5 billion in the first year. Such a large additional expenditure considerably complicated the case for decontrol, in that Congress had to consider not only the

TABLE 4.3 *Prices and Quantities for Natural Gas, 1965–77*

Year	Interstate regulated sales		Intrastate unregulated sales		Imported sales	
	Prices	Quantities	Prices	Quantities	Prices	Quantities
			(average annual rates of change)			
1965–69	1.2	6.5	2.8	6.7	0.3	14.3
1969–72	5.6	1.9	19.4	4.5	7.8	13.6
1972–77	27.5	−5.2	42.0	1.6	45.2	0.3

SOURCE: *Sales by Producers of Natural Gas to Interstate Pipeline Companies, 1972* (Washington, D.C.: FPC, June 1974). *Energy Data Reports: Interstate Gas Prices and Financial Data* (Washington, D.C.: DOE, Energy Information Administration, March 1978). Federal Energy Regulatory Commission (FERC) and FPC biannual and quarterly news releases on intrastate natural gas prices, 1957–77. *Department of Energy 1977 Annual Report to Congress*, vol. 3, and *Quarterly Report* (Washington, D.C.: Energy Information Administration, April 1978).

positive effect of reducing shortages but also the adverse political impact on the lawmakers of substantial price increases to current residential and commercial users. With these complications, the fifty cents was never allowed and the required increase grew each year.

The first step to catch up to excess demands was taken by the FPC in a comprehensive 1976 rate proceeding which allowed increases in new contract field prices of almost one dollar per MCF. This price hike, unthinkable five years earlier, was accomplished by using the existing process to derive estimates of the rate base and rate of return required to obtain additional supplies from new underground producing horizons. The source of estimates of the costs of these new supplies was data on sales of future production in the unregulated intrastate markets.

This move away from the orthodox regulatory process to forward-looking cost estimation involved legal controversies. The legal dispute was settled by Supreme Court review in *American Public Gas Company* v. *Federal Energy Regulatory Commission* (*FERC*) (555 F2d 852, 1977) which affirmed the authority of the regulatory agency to use forward estimates. Following this decision, there was significant new exploration and development activity as well as reduced growth in consumption as these price increases passed back into investment incentives and forward into wholesale and retail prices for delivered gas. Furthermore, there were no political or economic disruptions from the billion dollars of increased expenditures for each trillion cubic feet of additional gas going into regulated markets.

The examples of airline-passenger fare and natural-gas rate reform highlight the important role of commission initiatives in phasing out excess regulation. Congress merely followed the lead of these agencies in deregulating. But the issue raised by these internal reductions in controls is whether the process terminates in unregulated markets. By selectively decontrolling certain aspects of behavior, the sudden impact of the changes brought about by shifting to open markets has been reduced. But regulation has been prolonged and in the gas case extended by Congress once again. If prices at the end of the phasing turn out to be still too low, the transition will most likely continue so as to make regulation and phased decontrol indistinguishable.

Current Reform of Health and Safety Regulation

Changes in internal review processes could also affect the results from controls in the new regulatory agencies. The most important of these would be the requirement that there be some assessment of the results of regulation as part of the formulation of new standards. The Ford and Carter Administrations both proposed that major rule-makings be justified by findings that economy-wide gains from the new rules were significant. The inflation impact statement required by President Ford, and the economic impact statement required by President Carter,[3] in turn tried to set in motion procedures whereby agencies demonstrated substantial reductions in accidents, illness, or injuries from a rule-making decision. New rules also had to be shown to be less costly than alternative regulatory policies. Regulatory agencies such as EPA, OSHA, and NHTSA, since 1975, have been completing such findings and have provided projections on economy-wide impact of more health and safety as part of their rule-making records.

In theory, this new process should reduce, even eliminate, excessive regulation. The impact statement that shows an inability on the part of the agency to produce positive economy-wide impact should stand in the way of the issuance of excessive standards. But there is a vast difference between the best possible results from invoking such a policy and its practical effects. The inflation impact statement was not required of all federal agencies; the independent regulatory commissions were exempt, for instance. And, in fact, the carrying out of these procedures was substantively limited to a half-dozen agencies in the Office of the President. Furthermore, most of the statements were probably done as part of the justification process after decisions had been made, rather than as part of the preparatory work for making decisions on whether to invoke new regulations.

Only when the statement process moved outside the regulatory agencies were some changes possible in decision-making. In the case of OSHA safety standards for coke ovens in the steel industry, the Council on Wage and Price Stability (COWPS) as well as OSHA completed inflation impact statements. The analysis by COWPS differed widely with OSHA on the impact, with COWPS finding a significant and OSHA finding an insignificant adverse effect from the new standards. In the case of NHTSA decision-making with respect to the installation of safety air bags in automobiles, the process was opened up to allow estimates of impact by the automobile manufacturers and of the insurance companies and NHTSA staff. But in this case, as in the case of coke-oven standards, the final effect of the impact statement was to delay, without changing the nature of, the decision. The agencies went ahead with coke-oven standards and air-bag requirements even though they were estimated by opponents to be less than beneficial in the sense implied by the impact statement.[4]

Nevertheless, impact analyses have compelled agencies to take account of the economy-wide effects of their rule-makings and to defend this accounting. Impact statements may hinder further development of ineffective and costly equipment standards, even though they have not yet been sufficiently incorporated into decision-making to make regulation more effective in a general way.[5]

Reform by Court Decree

Recent court decisions evaluating the health and safety control process are an important new element in this regulation. Since regulation was established, the courts had, on appeal of agency rule-makings, been willing to determine the fairness of proceedings and whether there was factual support for agency conclusions in the record of the proceedings. This approach encouraged the building of lengthy dockets on equipment specifications, but it did not much affect the results of the rule-making process. In four recent OSHA cases, however, the federal judiciary, tentatively at first and then in a declarative way, began to evaluate the results from rule-making.

The four court decisions involved OSHA's benzene, coke-oven-emission, vinyl-chloride, and asbestos-dust standards. Each standard was a rule-making on maximum in-plant emissions and was part of the set of new rules for health rather than safety conditions in the workplace. Each was a physical limit on a substance to be applied at any plant location. The asbestos standard was the subject of review and here the court upheld consideration of economic feasibility in the promulgation of the standard.[6] At the same time, however, the court was guarded in its review of the impact of the standard for fear of infringing upon policy-making in the agency. The coke-oven and vinyl-chloride standards were reviewed as well, and again the court decisions essentially stopped short of reviewing the economic impact of the standards.[7]

With the decision on the benzene standard, however, the court made a significant departure from this position.[8] In this case, its review not only considered whether the economic feasibility of the benzene standard had been an issue, but explicitly used its own cost-benefit criterion to appraise the standard. Thus the court broke through the carefully preserved judicial distance of the previous cases and asserted itself much more directly and forcefully in appraising the worth of the standard.

The issues were first raised when in May of 1977 OSHA published a proposed permanent benzene standard that provided for a reduction in the airborne permissible exposure limit from 10 to 1 parts per million (ppm) and established requirements relating to dermal and eye contact, exposure monitoring, medical surveillance, methods of compliance, labeling, and record-keeping. This proposed standard was based on OSHA's determination that the available scientific evidence established that employee exposure to benzene presents a leukemia hazard and that exposure should be limited to the lowest feasible level. After holding hearings on the proposed standard, OSHA promulgated the benzene standard in February 1978. The American Petroleum Institute filed petitions for review of the standard in the U.S. Court of Appeals stating that the evidence did not show that the reduction of the exposure limit was reasonably necessary or appropriate to provide safe or healthful employment.

In response to the petition, the court held that the reduction of airborne permissible exposure limit from 10 to 1 ppm was to be set aside, "in the absence of substantial evidence indicating that measurable benefits to be achieved by the reduction of permissible exposure to benzene bore a reasonable relationship to the one-half billion dollar cost of such regulation for the affected industries." It was also decided that the dermal contact prohibition should be set aside, since the regulation was based on "dated, inconclusive data" and not on the latest scientific information.

The court noted in its decision that, although the OSHA statute requires the goal of attaining the highest degree of health and safety protection for the employee, "it does not give OSHA the unbridled discretion to adopt standards designed to create absolutely risk-free workplaces regardless of cost." In determining whether the benzene standard was reasonably necessary to protect workers from a hazard, the court was guided by the decision in *Aqua Slide 'N' Dive Corporation* v. *Consumer Product Safety Commission.*[9] Aqua Slide, which according to the court, "requires the agency to assess the benefits in light of the burdens to be imposed by the standard. Although the agency does not have to conduct an elaborate cost-benefit analysis, it does have to determine whether the benefits expected from the standard bear a reasonable relationship to the costs imposed by the standard."

Noting that OSHA had attempted to measure the expected costs of the standard, the court went on to determine that OSHA had failed in its obligation to show expected benefits to balance against these costs. Rather, OSHA had assumed that the benefits would be appreciable and could be achieved at a cost the industry could absorb. OSHA had "based this assumption on a finding that benzene was unsafe at any level and its conclusion that exposures to lower levels of toxic materials would be safer than exposure to higher levels." This was deficient because "substantial evidence does not support OSHA's conclusion that benefits are likely to be appreciable. Without an estimate of benefits supported by substantial evidence, OSHA is unable to justify a finding that the benefits to be realized from the standard bear a reasonable relationship to its one-half billion dollar price tag." Given this failure to provide an estimate of expected benefits from reducing the permissible exposure limit, the court argued that such a failure "makes it impossible to assess the reasonableness of the relationship between expected costs and benefits. This failure means that the required support is lacking to show reasonable necessity for the standard promulgated."

The results from this decision are uncertain, depending on whether it stands on review and whether other circuit courts adopt it is a precedent. Despite this uncertainty, the principle is far-reaching. As an approach to court review, the use of cost-benefit analysis on appeal could put an additional burden on OSHA to assess the effects of its standards and therefore could facilitate challenges to arbitrary or excessive on-the-job regulations.

On review of different issues related to equipment standards, another circuit court made finding benefits a direct responsibility of NHTSA as well. The case involved a mandated braking system for trucks and buses established by NHTSA's FMVSS 121, as originally adopted in January of 1973. This ruling established safety standards for air-brake systems by setting maximum stopping distances for vehicles at different speeds without locking wheels. Although the standard did not specify the technology to be used, it implied that an antilock device was necessary for large trucks in order to meet the requirement that stops be made without lock-up of wheels more than "momentarily" and the available device consisted of a computer attached to each axle of the tractor-trailer which sensed when a wheel began to lock and momentarily released the brake to regain traction. Serious questions soon arose as to the reliability and safety of this antilock device, because of relay valve failures, false warning signals, and failures of the warning signal required by NHTSA when the antilock was used. Radio frequency interference was also a problem, causing the antilock device to malfunction and the brakes to fail without warning. Among the problems attributed to the device were lateral instability, jackknifing, and wheel lock-up. Not infrequently drivers attempted to solve these myriad problems by simply deactivating the device.

In a court test of these standards, Paccar, Incorporated, and the American Trucking Association (ATA) contended that they did not meet the statutory requirement of practicability because no need was demonstrated for the air-brake standard, the cost of the system was high, and its requirements were beyond the reach of current technology. They also argued that it was not a reasonable standard since the failure of the antilock system—which they considered to be an unreliable device—created a potentially more dangerous situation than faced by vehicles with the old brake systems.

The truck brake case was decided in April 1978 in favor of Paccar and the ATA with the court holding that "in view of substantial evidence that 'in-use' performance of vehicles equipped with a brake 'anti-lock' was not consistent with performance required by the standard and may have been more hazardous in performance than prestandard vehicles, the agency's failure to conduct more intensive testing of vehicles certified under the standard was an illegal abuse of discretion." It was noted that NHTSA had relied upon testimony of some manufacturers, the lack of reports of highway accidents attributed to the antilock, and the testing of three tractor-trailers from June until September 1975. In the court's opinion, "more probative and convincing data evidencing the reliability and safety of vehicles that are equipped with antilock and in use must be available before the agency can enforce a standard requiring its installation.''

On appeal of this decision, NHTSA argued that the role of a court reviewing an administrative decision is limited, and that the Circuit Court in this case had extended beyond this role. NHTSA boldly stated that in its opinion "the decision in this case amounts to a substitution of judicial for administrative judgment in a manner repeatedly condemned by this court and other courts of appeal.'' The agency position on this matter was denied by the Court of Appeals and NHTSA published a notice in the *Federal Register* interpreting the Court of Appeals' decision to mean that the no-lock portions of the standard were invalidated insofar as they applied to trucks and trailers. [10]

The OSHA and NHTSA case decisions both redirected these agencies away from rule-makings requiring equipment on feasibility grounds alone to standards justified on the grounds that the total economic and social performance of the regulated companies under the new regulations will be improved. Those aspects of performance would include accident reduction, improvement in health, and greater product quality. Whether such changes can be translated into economic benefits is problematical. But the making of estimates of the extent to which lives were saved or products were rendered more useful would greatly improve the foundations for an effective regulatory decision-making process. By adopting the court's line of reasoning, these agencies could reduce the high-cost, low-benefit results from health and safety regulation.

Proposals for More Effective Regulatory Reform

While the reform process has not been without its accomplishments, the overall record falls short of what is needed to reverse recent declines in performance caused by controls in the regulated industries. Beyond regulatory lag and inefficiency, the poor results reflect the inevitable end product of the present administrative procedures. The critical step toward improving the present condition of the regulated industries would be to develop better administrative processes in the agencies responsibile for both price controls and health and safety regulation. Because price regulation uses past-period estimates of costs to establish future revenues, the companies involved would still be pricing behind current cost and demand conditions even if rate cases could be decided immediately. Because health and safety regulation centers on equipment standards, the case-making process has moved in directions that keep cost increases the same across companies and allows them to be passed on in price increases. Because the equipment and process changes have been the same across companies, while health and safety conditions varied widely, the controls applied to the least safe and most polluting companies could not have been effective. This process almost necessarily avoids any general impact on social conditions.

Three kinds of changes are required to transform given administrative practices into productive regulation. The first would be to invoke price regulations that applied profit constraints based on current and future costs of investments for providing service. The second would be to deregulate where conditions of competition, service quality, and the economy no longer justified any control process. The third, in health and safety regulation, would be to require a procedure for assessing results or economic effects in rule-making.

The establishment of a process of current-cost rate control would require federal and state legislation. One way would have the commissions permit immediate rate increases when requested, subject to later repayment by the company of excess profits to consumers. The basis for determining excess profits would be estimates of revenues and costs from the period in which the higher rates were in effect. Thus the review of a rate increase proposal requested in 1984 would occur in 1985, and would use data on actual 1984 operating and capital costs and revenues. A process that compared the same year's costs and receipts would replace the method by which past costs are used to set limits on future revenues. The new process would be, in fact, the same as that now used by municipal electric power companies not subject to rate regulation but rather to bond-issue regulations requiring excess returns to be repaid to rate-payers. This way of regulating would not only eliminate the adverse effects of regulatory lag in case reviews but also, by use of contemporaneous data on costs and demands, reduce the inaccuracy of capital cost estimates.

The elimination of rate controls should proceed on a case-by-case basis, with Congress bearing the burden of proof for continuing price and entry regulation in the transportation and energy industries. The cases for the airlines, motor-freight carriers, and railroads would likely be decided against continued regulation. These industries were regulated in the past for a variety of reasons, with highly adverse effects. Promoting industry profitability—and therefore service competition and growth—was a good reason for regulation in the 1940s and 1950s in the early development of these industries. With these service concerns no longer so urgent, what is needed now is the complete elimination of rate control.

Examination of electricity, gas, and telephone retail regulation would show the need to continue some present controls, particularly those over gas retail prices and telephone residence services where there are not competitive sources of supply. Controls would still be justified over the local monopolies providing electricity service, so as to keep prices below unregulated levels (but not down to present levels). Thus to some extent this review would acknowledge the need for forward-looking rate setting.

The railroads, airlines, and gas-producing companies are now operating under phased deregulation. Further efforts along these lines should be institutionalized by legislation abolishing the ICC and FPC (now the FERC) at this stage of decontrol. Peremptory legislation is also needed to eliminate state regulatory agency control of the motor-freight carriers. The legislation should specify a decontrol objective and should set general guidelines for the steps to be taken in the decontrol process. With the civil servants motivated by legislation to meet standards for the elimination of their own activities, the decontrol goal could be achieved in time to restore these industries to reasonable levels of productivity, growth, and progress.

The further institutionalization of performance analysis is the most important step that can be taken to improving health and safety regulations. Once made central to the process, the analyses would contain estimates of those costs imposed on the economy by the proposed regulatory activities, and of the magnitudes of the positive effects of these activities. Effects would be measured in dollar terms whenever possible, but where they include nonmonetary benefits which cannot be put in those terms, they would have to be measured on other dimensions.

The part of institutionalization that counts is integration of the analysis into the decision-making process. This is done when the agency has to consider economy-wide costs and benefits from its rule-making, when others have to be given the opportunity to interject their estimates of those effects, and when the review courts can then take a hard look at how widely and thoroughly the agency considered those effects. At that point decision-makers have the burden of proving that any extension of regulation would improve upon present conditions in that industry and elsewhere in the economy. The burden would almost certainly be too great to allow most of the excessive regulations in EPA, NHTSA, or OSHA to expand along the present lines of practice.

Prospects for Reform

In recent years, all presidents and most members of Congress have promised to bring an end to excessive regulation in the United States. Members of the House and Senate have acted on these commitments by dealing with bills calling for decontrol in particular industries, for termination or sunset processes to apply to all regulatory agencies, and for new procedures in major rule-markings that would require the agency to show that their rules were beneficial to the economy and society as a whole. But little has come of this as substantive proposals in other than airlines have fallen by the wayside.

The question for the 1980s is whether it will be possible to reform regulation along lines of the three important initiatives. Can we actually by new statute (1) reduce the backwardness of public-utility price setting, (2) deregulate, and (3) require impact analyses in proposed new health and safety regulations? From all appearances, regardless of the abundance of reform rhetoric, the answer is that such changes are unlikely. The most important reason for this state of affairs is that real regulatory change is impolitic.

The recent adverse effects from regulation have been that investment and output growth have been curtailed. The case for legislative reform has been essentially that regulation should be reduced or eliminated so as to add to the profitability of new investment and thereby add to capacity and output growth. But this requires higher prices and less safety equipment. The increase in rates to established consumers and the reduction in observable safety equipment would be resisted as a matter of course, even though these changes would benefit consumers some years hence when investment has increased. The trade-off by new statute of direct price increases or reduced safety equipment now for indirect output increases later would be highly unlikely. Indeed, not only is it unlikely, but where the adverse effects from regulation are most extensive and therefore the direct price increases or equipment reductions from reform would be the greatest, there would be the least convincing political case for legislative reform.

In the 1980s the American economy will probably continue to operate under the legislation on regulation much as it now exists on the statute books. As a result, the economy will not perform as well as it might and, more likely than not, there will be some shortages or disruptions of service in the regulated industries. But the pervasive result from the activities of the agencies will not be such shortages; rather, there will continue to be reductions in the growth of the quantity and quality of goods and services throughout the economy. As regulatory practices and rules expand, the agencies, boards, and commissions will reduce the returns from and opportunities for capital and output growth. If inflation is extensive, the growth rates of the price-regulated industries will be reduced the most. This growth effect will be transformed to lower-quality services, lower rates of expansion of service to outlying groups of consumers, and less introduction of technologically superior equipment and systems to those now receiving service. At the same time, those goods and services provided by the industries most affected by health, safety, and environmental regulation will be more expensive, less satisfactory in performance and less likely to improve over time.

This future condition of the regulated industries does not make the outlook for the rest of the economy very promising. The reduced growth of the energy, transportation, and communications industries will raise costs of manufacturing and trade, causing their growth rates also to be reduced. Reduced growth in the metals, materials, and automobile industries from health and environmental regulations will slow down the economy as well. And there are not going to be gains in more safety or better health to compensate for the rising costs of EPA, NHTSA, and OSHA regulation given the present ways of setting equipment and performance standards.

This is to say that improvements in the performance of the regulated industries is central to realizing an impressive rate of development of the economy as a whole. Yet reform is not a promising prospect, since what is gained is very indirectly related to long-term development of the economy, and what is given up po-

litically by proposing reform is directly shown to be more stable prices and more safety equipment now. To continue regulatory practices on present lines is likely; but to do so is to deprive the economy of goals and services, for little if anything in return.

Notes

CHAPTER 1

1. The Ford Administration's Aviation Act of 1975 (Senate Bill 2551) proposed to remove rate and entry regulation, and the Motor Carrier Reform Act of 1975 (House Resolution 10,909) proposed greater rate flexibility, easier entry, and elimination of regulations requiring empty backhauls, underloading, and circuitous routes. Also proposed was the Financial Institutions Act of 1975 (Senate Bill 1267) to increase interbank competition, to raise ceilings on interest rates payable to depositors, and to permit expansion of banking services now contrary to the regulations. Gas deregulation proposals were made as part of. the Energy Independence Act of 1975, initiated by President Ford on January 30, 1975 (Senate Bill 59).

The Consumer Goods Pricing Act of 1975 (December 12, 1975) stated that state laws which permitted producers to set minimum prices for brand-name products at retail would be in violation of federal antitrust laws. This legislation nullified the Miller-Tydings Act of 1937 and the McGuire Act of 1952, which had provided antitrust exemptions. Fair-trade laws had restricted competition among retailers through what the Judiciary Committee called "legalized price fixing." The committee estimated that fair-trade raised prices of certain consumer goods 18 to 27 percent over those in free-trade states.

The Railroad Revitalization and Regulatory Reform Act of 1976 (Public Law 94-210), gave railroads more discretion on lowering rates where the individual road did not have "market dominance." Stock brokerage fees were dealt with in the Securities Act Amendments of 1975 (Public Law 94-145), which was signed into law June 4, 1975. The law abolished fixed commission rates and minimum commissions agreed to by members of the Stock Exchange, thereby increasing competition among brokers carrying out stock sale transactions.

The Airline Deregulation Act of 1978 (Public Law 95-504) phases out controlled fares over the period 1979–83. The Natural Gas Policy Act of 1978 (Public Law 95-621), while involving a large number of different schedules, follows roughly the same time schedule. There has been considerable controversy as to whether at the end of the phasing period controls will disappear or be reinstated by Congress.

2. This estimate is contained in "The 'Regulators,' They Cost you $130 Billion a Year," *U.S. News and World Report* (June 30, 1975), pp. 24–28. "High" and "low" costs were estimated for each regulatory program. Simple addition of the lower set of values yielded a cost to the public of $105 billion, while addition of upper limits produced costs of $130 billion. Specific industry regulation—encompassing transportation, labor, energy, agriculture, financial institutions, foreign and domestic trade practices—had costs of $45 to $60 billion a year, while environmental regulation cost $50 to $60 billion a year, and health and safety and product quality regulation imposed an annual cost of more than $10 billion. These estimates were derived from the U.S. Office of Management and Budget, White House, and other official sources.

3. Murray L. Weidenbaum and Robert DeFina estimate regulatory costs in "The Cost of Federal Regulation of Economic Activity," American Enterprise Institute Reprint No. 88. The authors conclude that regulation imposed a total cost of $66 billion on the American economy in 1976. Specific industry controls cost $20 billion in the same year, while the cost of financial regulation was estimated at just over $1 billion. Energy and environmental regulation cost over $8 billion and federal control of job safety added $4 billion to costs of operations. Finally, government regulation of consumer safety and health cost the public over $6 billion. Weidenbaum and DeFina also estimate a cost for paperwork associated with regulation. They allege that such paperwork costs $25 billion in 1976. The source is given as follows: "The basic approach followed in the study was to cull from the available literature the more reliable estimates of the costs from specific regulatory programs, to put these estimates on a consistent and reliable basis, and to aggregate the results for 1976."

Paul Sommers, in *The Economic Costs of Regulation: Report for the American Bar Association, Commission on Law and the Economy* (Department of Economics, Yale University, January 1978) finds the annual cost of regulation to be between $58 and $73 billion. Sommers derives regulatory costs for 11 sectors of the economy, which in turn can be roughly grouped into three categories: (1) economic, (2) environmental, and (3) health, safety, and product quality regulation. The cost of economic regulation is said to be $11.6 to $12.3 billion, as a result of regulatory inducements of gas shortages, abnormal price fluctuations, and resource waste. Beyond measuring costs, Sommers indicates that such regulation results in a rate of return to electric power companies so low that there is a capital equipment or capacity shortage, and thereby a potential 7 percent GNP loss during the consequent service interruptions. Environmental regulation costs the public $13 billion in higher automobile costs. By far the largest regulatory cost to the economy, $30 to $45 billion, stems from regulation of health, safety, and product quality. Sommers estimates "investments for universal compliance with health and safety standards" at between $17 and $31.5 billion. Like many regulatory cost studies, the Sommers report "draws mainly on the published academic literature, with some recourse to readily available government documents."

Unlike other studies, Sommers attempts to measure the benefits of regulation, thus lowering the assessment of "negative impact" of regulation on the economy. For example, Sommers sets the administrative cost of telephone regulation at $37.6 million, but he also points out that this cost is "possibly offset by the benefits of lower rates." The "cost" estimates given for Sommers are net of consumer and worker benefits of lower prices, cleaner air, and lower accident rates.

4. The Motor Carrier Act (S1629), part II, Declaration of Policy.

5. *House of Representatives Report Number 2254,* Civil Aeronautics Bill (75th Cong., 1st sess.), p. 2.

6. Public Law 73-416, section 1 (June 19, 1934) as found in *U.S. Statutes,* vol. 48, part 1, p. 1,064.

7. Other regulatory agencies were established to provide consumers with both information and protection against deceptive practices, particularly in financial markets. These were well established by the end of the 1930s, although there also have been recent additions to this group (see Appendix Table A.3). Agencies regulating financial institutions control entry and competition in ways designed to reduce the likelihood of bank failure, thereby enhancing investor confidence in the system. The Securities and Exchange Commission (SEC) was established to protect securities holders against fraud while regulating brokers so as to expand services to small shareholders. The addition of several new agencies in the 1970s was justified in part because the SEC did not provide sufficient service. For instance, the Securities Investors Protection Commission (SIPC) requires insurance against stock losses, and the Commodity Futures Trading Commission (CFTC) extends SEC-type coverage to the futures market. Furthermore, existing agencies have modified their regulatory emphases in recent years. One of the largest, the Federal Trade Commission (FTC), has redirected its activities in the last decade from an emphasis on the suppression of deceptive practices to the restructuring of concentrated industries by bringing court cases in markets where there is alleged "shared monopoly" among the largest companies. The regulation here proceeds in ways common to both price and safety regulation, with price levels set and product or service specifications also determined in agency proceedings.

8. The source for this estimate is a staff paper prepared for the Sub-Committee on Oversight and Investigations of the House Committee on Interstate and Foreign Commerce by the Office of Economic Analysis of the Office of Program Analysis, U.S. Government Accounting Office, *An Economic Evaluation of the OMB Paper on "The Costs of Regulation and Restrictive Practices"* (Washington, D.C.: U.S. Government Printing Office, 1975).

9. Administrative Procedure Act, 5 U.S. Code 551 et seq. and 701 et seq. (1976).

10. As early as 1936, the Supreme Court (in *St. Joseph Stockyards Company* v. *United States,* 298 US 38 at 49–50 [1936]) said that "the Judicial inquiry into the facts goes no further than to ascertain whether there is evidence to support the find-

ings, and the question of the weight of the evidence in determining issues of fact lies with the legislative agency acting within its statutory authority. But the Constitution fixes limits to the ratemaking power by prohibiting the deprivation of property without due process of law or the taking of private property for public use without just compensation.'' Thus the Court maintained the right to examine the weight of the evidence when the question concerned confiscation of private property. Present-day judicial practices have promoted to a much greater extent the strict application of legislative directives. This conclusion is Professor Stewart's: ''By undertaking a more searching scrutiny of the substantiality of the evidence supporting agency fact-finding and by insisting on a wide range of procedural safeguards, the courts have required agencies to adhere more scrupulously to legislative directive'' (Richard B. Stewart, ''The Reformation of American Administrative Law,'' *Harvard Law Review* 88 [1975]: 1,671, with reference to *Universal Camera Corporation* v. *NLRB*, 340 US 474 [1951] and *W. Y. Sung* v. *McGrath* 339 US 33 [1950]).

CHAPTER 2

1. A general formula for the regulated limit on revenues is $p \cdot q = \propto$ $c + d + r \cdot B/(1\text{-}t)$ where p is the price or rate level on sales of q, c is total operating costs, d is depreciation, and $r \cdot B/ (1\text{-}t)$ equals total allowed profit returns before taxes at the tax rate, t, and at the fair rate of return, r, on rate base B of undepreciated investment. The estimates of c and d are based on accounting data for some recent test period of operations and, as such, are not significantly controversial. But $r \cdot B$ contains two subjective estimates, the fair rate of return, r, and the company's undepreciated capital base, B, which because they are subjective and judgmental could exceed costs and then be compounded by multiplication. It is in determining the r and B factors in capital returns that the regulatory review in practice effectively constrains company decisions.

2. This requires a determination of what has to be paid in interest and dividends, and what increases in stock prices are necessary in order to be able to issue additional securities. The required interest rates are indicated by the coupon values and the prices of that company's outstanding bond issues; but the fair rate of return on stock cannot so easily be estimated from market observations. The necessary rate of return on equity capital—that is, the expected return on an investment of comparable risk—cannot be found directly from a company's stock share earnings-price ratio, because not only do investors' present expected returns but also investors' expectations of the future rate of growth of earnings determine the stock's price. That is, an investor holding stock in the regulated company has the expectation of earning a rate of return equal to $(d + \Delta p)/p + g$, where d is dividends, p is stock price, Δp is the change in stock price, and g is the expected rate of growth of dividends. If this rate of return falls short of those expected for other investments of the same risk, then stockholders will sell, reducing the company's stock price, p, until the rate is comparable for the coming period. Thus the com-

pany should be allowed to earn enough to establish comparable levels of p, d, and g. But the g term is not directly observable from recent market behavior. Thus the commissions cannot depend on current or past earnings data to insure objective statistical estimates of costs of equity capital. See Stuart C. Myers, "The Application of Finance Theory to Public Utility Rate Cases," *The Bell Journal of Economics and Management Science* (Spring 1972), pp. 58–97.

3. Paul L. Joskow, "Pricing Decisions of Regulated Firms: A Behavioral Approach," *The Bell Journal of Economics and Management Science* (Autumn 1973), pp. 118–40.

4. Paul L. Joskow, "The Determination of the Allowed Rate of Return in a Formal Regulatory Hearing," *The Bell Journal of Economics and Management Science* (Autumn 1972), pp. 632–44.

5. The case-decision process on fair profits results in significant curtailment of the frequency of price changes because commissions sometimes have ordered reductions when increases were requested. There is thus always some chance that a company will leave a case review with lower prices than if there had been no review at all. Given this risk, the companies have asked for price increases only when capital costs have increased significantly. As a result, the process not only generates stable prices, but also fewer reductions than would occur with some other kind of regulation or with an unregulated market.

6. Thomas G. Moore, "The Effectiveness of Regulation of Electric Utility Prices," *Southern Economic Journal* (April 1970), pp. 365–75. The purpose of this study was to measure the effectiveness of regulation in reducing prices to residential users of electricity. A weighted average marginal cost was computed for 62 private electric and 7 municipal companies, based on the average cost of production of the marginal plant. By regression analysis, the demands at various prices were estimated for each firm and, from these demands and marginal costs, estimates were made of profit-maximizing unregulated prices. The author then compared these with actual regulated prices to assess the effectiveness of regulation.

Raymond Jackson, "Regulation and Electric Utility Rate Levels," *Land Economics* (August 1969), pp. 372–76. Jackson, using multiple-regression techniques to isolate the impact of regulation, analyzed the effectiveness of state commissions in reducing the average price per KWH paid by residential and industrial users by comparing regulated and unregulated utilities which served cities of 50,000 for the years 1940, 1950, and 1960. His equation included five determinants of electric rates: $AR' = a_0 + a_1 P' + a_2 Y' + a_3 F' + a_4 H' + a_5 R'$ where AR' is average revenue per KWH, P' is population in cities of 50,000 or over served by the utility, Y' is income level of the population, F' is fuel costs, H' is proportion of electricity produced by hydroelectric power, R' is the regulation variable set equal to 1 when the utility is regulated and 0 when unregulated. The coefficients of the regulatory variable were negative in all three test years for equations with AR' separately for total sales, residential sales, and commercial and industrial sales. However, a statistically significant effect from regulation on the rate level was observed for total sales only in 1950 and 1960. For residential sales, a marginally significant effect on rates from regulation occurred in 1960 but not in either 1940 or 1950. But the regression results indicate that regulation had a significant impact in lowering commercial and industrial rates: "The regulation coefficient is significant for commercial and industrial sales . . . [suggesting] that regulatory commissions have succeeded in protecting the interests of the industrial and commercial users whose demand for electricity is more elastic than the residential consumer and are less in need of such protection" (p. 376).

George J. Stigler and Claire Friedland, "What Can Regulators Regulate? The Case of Electricity," *Journal of Law and Economics* (October 1962), pp. 1–16. Also R. K. Davidson, *Price Discrimination in Selling Gas and Electricity* (Baltimore: Johns Hopkins University Press, 1955), and Twentieth Century Fund, *Electric Power and Government Policy* (New York, 1948). Earlier reviews of this research literature were provided in R. E. Caves, "Rate Regulation and Market Performance in the American Economy," *American Economic Review* (May 1964), and in R. C. Cramden, "The Effectiveness of Economic Regulation: A Legal View," *American Economic Review* (May 1964), pp. 182–91.

7. Raymond Jackson, "Regulation and Electric Utility Rate Levels."

8. See the Federal Communications Commission Report, FCC Docket 20,003, where it is stated that "the telephone industry contends that so-called 'specialized' services such as private line service and terminal equipment leasing presently generate revenues substantially in excess of their direct costs, which help to defray overall system costs and thus to maintain low rates for basic telephone service" (p. 768).

9. S. C. Littlechild and J. J. Rousseau, "Pricing Policy of a U.S. Telephone Company," *Journal of Public Economics* 4 (February 1975): 35–56.

10. Paul W. MacAvoy and Roger Noll, "Relative Prices on Regulated Transactions of the Natural Gas Pipelines," *The Bell Journal of Economics and Management Science* (Spring 1973), pp. 212–34.

11. Stanislaw Wellisz, "Regulation of Natural Gas Pipelines: An Economic Analysis," *Journal of Political Economy* (February 1963), pp. 30–41. Also see his "The Public Interest in Gas Industry Rate Structure," *Public Utilities Fortnightly* (July 19, 1962, and August 2, 1962), pp. 65–78 and 145–56.

12. Alfred C. Aman and Glenn S. Howard, "Natural Gas and Electric Utility Rate Reform: Taxation through Ratemaking?" *Hastings Law Journal* (May 1977), p. 1,122.

13. William A. Jordan, "Producer Protection, Prior Market Structure and the Effects of Government Regulation," *The Journal of Law and Economics* (April 1972), pp. 151–76 (quotation from p. 163).

14. Ibid., p. 167.

15. Of course, higher fares can reduce total revenues (and profits) if demand is sufficiently elastic. This appears not to have been the case in these industries at that time, except perhaps for the railroads.

16. Jordan, p. 172.

17. Promotion of service and stability of industry structure had been important objectives of regulation of the domestic commercial airlines. The Federal Aviation Act of 1958 (49 USC Chapter 1302 or: Public Law 85-726, Title 1, S. 102, Aug.

23, 1958, 72 Stat. 740.) required that the CAB discharge its duties in a way that considered the public interest and "the public convenience and necessity" but required (a) "encouragement and development of an air-transportation system properly adapted to the present and future needs of the foreign and domestic commerce of the United States," of the Postal Service, and of the national defense at the same time that it should (b) "recognize and preserve the inherent advantages of, assure the highest degree of safety in, and foster sound economic conditions in, such transportation." There was in the next subsection a requirement for the (c) "promotion of adequate, economical, and efficient service by air carriers at reasonable charges, without unjust discriminations, undue preference or advantages, or unfair or destructive competitive practices." The potential conflict was with the "development of an air-transportation system" that was larger than possible at "reasonable charges" and therefore required higher fares than those normally found in competitive markets or even under conditions of rate-base rate-of-return regulation in the public utility industries.

18. G. W. Douglas and J. C. Miller, III, *Economic Regulation of Domestic Air Transport: Theory and Policy* (Washington, D.C.: The Brookings Institution, 1974).

19. Richard E. Caves, *Air Transport and Its Regulators: An Industry Study* (Cambridge, Mass.: Harvard University Press, 1962).

20. Michael Conant, *Railroad Mergers and Abandonments* (Berkeley: University of California Press, 1965), p. 132.

21. James C. Nelson, in "The Effects of Entry Control in Surface Transport" (*Transportation Economics* [New York: The National Bureau of Economic Research, 1965], pp. 415–16), noted that "supporters of current regulation . . . strongly claim that it results in improved service, greater financial responsibility to shippers, and greater public safety on the highways. . . . Acknowledging that even regulated carriers prefer to serve points generating substantial traffic, the Commission indicated that 'in some instances' it had imposed a duty of serving small intermediate points by including them in a carrier's certificate even though an authorization was not sought."

22. Jordan, "Producer Protection, Prior Market Structures and the Effects of Government Regulation."

23. *Economic Report of the President* (Washington, D.C.: U.S. Government Printing Office, January 1978), Table B-65, "Bond Yields and Interest Rates, 1929–1977."

24. Changes in interest costs, which were more than 100 basis points over the period, are used here as a surrogate for changes in the costs of capital (where the total includes equity and depreciation costs as well). There are no useful series for these other components of capital costs, so that percentage changes in interest costs have to be used as an indicator of movement in all such costs.

25. These margins were high in the early 1960s, even given rising capital costs, because the regulated companies had substantial gains in productivity due to investment in improved equipment and to economies of larger-scale operations. During the early 1960s, the electricity, gas, telephone companies, and airlines all

had productivity growth half again greater than the average of the unregulated service industries (as indicated in Appendix P). Although the pattern of higher productivity continued for these industries in the last half of the decade, productivity growth rates did fall off for all of these industries except telephones and they stayed low for the trucking industry. With the loss of a point or two of growth of output per unit of labor resources, costs began to rise for the regulated companies as factor prices and other product prices increased in 1968 and thereafter.

26. Rates of return on the book value of assets are shown in Appendix C. These returns are calculated as the sum of the interest, dividends, and stock price appreciation divided by the beginning year market value of outstanding stocks and bonds. These return rates in the early 1960s did not differ from those on investments in the unregulated industries. Some investors' returns were higher, such as in airlines and motor freight, where expectations of rapid growth in demand led to substantial increases in stock prices. Others were lower, as in gas transmission, given predictions of a slowdown in the growth of gas-field supplies. Of the seven regulated industries four showed excess and three showed deficient returns relative to the market of all such investments.

27. *Phillips Petroleum Company* v. *Wisconsin,* 225 US 625 (1954).

28. The reopening of the case late in the decade, however, raised the ceiling by about 25 percent.

29. The commission further distorted the results toward price fixity by using average rather than marginal costs. Natural gas produced from a limited inventory has always been increasingly more costly to obtain as reserves have been depleted, so that marginal costs have to be greater than the average costs of finding and developing market supplies. Prices set equal to average costs fail to compensate for additional supplies, so that exploration and development is cut back. The commission tried to prevent this and thus to take account of higher costs at the margin by adding onto the average historical costs of finding gas an average premium for new discoveries. In the Permian Basin proceedings, this premium was approximately one cent per MCF in the ceiling price. This difference while important in principle was insubstantial in practice.

30. *Economic Report of the President* (Washington, D.C.: U.S. Government Printing Office, January 1978), Table B-2, B-37, B-55, B-56; and *Economic Report of the President* (January 1976), Table B-2, (decline from 1973 peak to 1975 trough).

31. Profit returns on book value remained much the same for these industries in the 1970s as in the early and middle 1960s, with railroads and airlines again below average rates of return. These estimates are given in Appendix C.

32. Paul L. Joskow, "Inflation and Environmental Concern: Structural Changes in the Process of Public Utility Price Regulation," *Journal of Law and Economics* (October 1974); and Roger Noll, "The Economics and Politics of Regulation," *Virginia Law Review* 57 (September 1971): 1,016–32.

33. The regulatory lag effects were estimated by fitting coefficients for the major cost factors, assuming a constant (or constant-rate-of-change) technology so that the contributions to the costs of output of each input cost factor remain constant

over time. The general form of the equations is: (1) PRICE $= a_0 + a_1$ FUEL $+ a_2$ WAGES $+ a_3$ CAPITAL $+ u$, where PRICE is the regulated price level (generally the Consumer Price Index for the product), FUEL is the Wholesale Price Index for the type(s) of fuel used by the industry, WAGES is the level of average hourly earnings of production workers in the industry, and CAPITAL is a composite of interest rates and construction or equipment costs faced by the industry. An expected price level (PRICEHAT) is estimated from use of the estimated coefficients as follows: (2) PRICEHAT $= a_0 + a_1$ FUEL $+ a_2$ WAGES $+ a_3$ CAPITAL. The estimated PRICEHAT is regressed on the actual PRICE and the pattern of residuals v was examined. Where v is (3) $v = $ PRICEHAT $- b_0 + b_1$ PRICE, the average v equal to zero occurred five quarters after a significant change in the halves of the cost variables occurred.

34. This hypothesis has been tested by comparing the rates of change of regulated prices with the rates of change of input costs. In theory, the magnitudes of price changes should fall behind cost changes, if regulatory lag and money illusion are operative. That is, prices should fall more slowly than costs during the early period and lag behind rising costs during the later period. To make such comparisons, equations were fitted with data on prices and costs in five industries. An expected rate was calculated for the entire period (pre- and post-inflation) as a whole. The differences between this expected rate and actual rates confirmed the existence of regulatory lag and money illusion for these industries in the late 1960s and early 1970s.

35. The initiation of price and allocation controls over petroleum products in the middle 1970s should be examined and the effects of the new controls documented, but unfortunately the research literature is not sufficiently broad and empirically based to establish firm conclusions on these matters at this time. The crude-oil price controls initiated after the OPEC embargo set ceiling prices on old oil at 1972 levels while leaving prices on new oil uncontrolled. After a number of administrative and legislative changes, mostly in the 1975 Energy Policy and Conservation Act, a three-tiered pricing system emerged with both old and new oil prices set at controlled levels and with only stripper-well production remaining uncontrolled. At the same time, refinery yield controls, regional gasoline allocation, and the timing of retail price increases were all regulated for the first time. The research literature establishes that controls probably reduced domestic crude-oil exploration and production. This increased domestic refinery output due to lower effective marginal costs for crude oil, and also increased crude oil imports to meet refinery input needs (a dissenting view has been offered by Milton Friedman and Professors C. F. Phelps and R. F. Smith, to the effect that refined product prices have not been reduced by regulation). The effects on the economy were to utilize excessive resources to purchase crude oil on the world market and to overuse resources in refining because of the bias built into regulation toward small refiners. But the magnitude of such waste, and the impact these changes have had on investment and GNP growth over the long run, have not been assessed in the research literature. Thus it is not possible here to compare the effects of crude-oil regulation with those elsewhere. The major references are: S. W. Chapel, ''The Oil Entitlements

Program and Its Effects on the Domestic Refining Industry," Rand Corporation Study P5717; J. C. Cox and A. W. Wright, "The Effects of Crude Oil Price Controls, Entitlements and Taxes on Refined Product Prices and Energy Independence," *Land Economics* (February 1978), pp. 1–15; R. E. Hall and R. S. Pindyck, "The Conflicting Goals of National Energy Policy," *The Public Interest* (Spring 1977), pp. 3–15; W. D. Montgomery, "A Case Study of Regulatory Programs of the Federal Energy Administration," *Social Science Working Paper Number 147*, California Institute of Technology (1977); C. E. Phelps and R. F. Smith, "Petroleum Regulation: The False Dilemma of Decontrol," Number R-1951-RC (January 1977), The Rand Corporation (1977); Milton Friedman, "Two Economic Fallacies," *Newsweek* (May 12, 1975), p. 83, and "Subsidizing OPEC Oil," *Newsweek* (June 23, 1975), p. 75.

36. Paul W. MacAvoy and Paul L. Joskow, "Regulation and the Financial Condition of the Electric Power Companies in the 1970s," *American Economic Review* (May 1975).

37. Ibid.

38. Donaldson, Lufkin, and Jenrette Securities Corporation, *Domestic Trunk Airlines: A Shortage Industry in the Making* (New York, June 1976).

39. Richard C. Levin, "Regulation, Barriers to Exit, and Railroad Investment Behavior." Paper presented at the National Bureau of Economic Research Conference on Public Regulation, Washington, D.C., December 15–17, 1977.

40. See Jeffrey Rohlffs, *Economically Efficient Bell System Pricing,* Attachment H. AT & T's submission to Congressman T. Van Deerlin, October 31, 1978. Dr. Rohlffs estimates marginal costs and rates for classes of service in ways that make these orders-of-magnitude differences quite likely.

CHAPTER 3

1. Ralph Nader, *Unsafe At Any Speed: The Designed-in Dangers of the American Automobile* (New York: Grossman, 1965); Rachel L. Carson, *Silent Spring* (Boston: Houghton Mifflin, 1962).

2. See National Traffic and Motor Vehicle Safety Act of 1966, Public Law 89-563, September 9, 1966, 80 STAT 718; see Senate Report No. 1301, 89th Cong., 2d Sess., 1966, p. 6.

3. The Senate Report in 1966 required that "every standard be stated in objective terms" within a short time period. See *The 1967 Annual Report of the National Highway Safety Agency in the Department of Commerce,* p. 50. The Senate had made it clear, however, at the time of the passage of the statute that the regulation was to be conducted through the issuance of performance standards rather than design or equipment standards: "Both the interim standards and the new and revised standards are expected to be performance standards, specifying the required minimum safe performance of vehicles but not the manner in which the manufacturer is to achieve the specified performance" (89th Cong., 2d Sess., June 23, 1966, p. 6). This was intended to avoid rigidities created by regulation in the

design of equipment and to promote technological advancement. For technical reasons and in order to prevent the growth of large bureaucracies, the conference report stated that "the Secretary is not to become involved in questions of design" (House Report No. 1919, 89th Cong., 2d Sess., 1966, p. 15).

4. *U.S. Code of Regulations,* Title 29, Section 1910.25 (b) (3) (ii).

5. Standard-setting to protect health rather than safety was only begun in OSHA's first five years. During the summer of 1973, OSHA issued emergency standards on pesticides and cancer-causing chemicals. The first standard protected agricultural workers against the toxic effects of 21 pesticides, specifying the time which must elapse before an employee may reenter the sprayed area. The second standard protected workers from 14 carcinogens. Precautions included "(1) prohibiting use of toilet facilities and drinking fountains inside a controlled area; (2) prohibiting smoking, smoking materials, food beverages in controlled areas; (3) posting warning signs, etc." (*Job, Safety and Health* [July 1973], p. 21). In May 1974, OSHA proposed a permanent standard stating that "workers should not be exposed to any detectable level of vinyl chloride, a cancer-causing chemical widely used in the plastics industry" ("New Standard: Vinyl Chloride," *Job, Safety and Health* [July 1974], p. 9). During the fall of 1975 new health standards were introduced regulating asbestos, toluene, alkyl benzenes, ketones, cyclohexane, and ozone. The exposure limit to asbestos was reduced as was exposure time to toluene. Requirements were set for medical examinations, record-keeping, monitoring workplace air, and training employees using toluene. More recently, in late 1977, OSHA proposed new standards for more suspected carcinogens. A rule-making procedure was established for removing carcinogens from the workplace. Depending on the severity of the findings from data analysis on cancer incidence, OSHA would issue either a temporary emergency order until a permanent standard could be issued or would hold public hearings before standards were set. All of these steps in health regulation have been for the purpose of developing a set of standards comparable in scope and magnitude to those in the consensus set of safety regulations. Since they cover very few substances and their scope is limited to emergency coverage in a number of cases, no detailed and comprehensive assessment of OSHA health regulation can be undertaken at this time.

6. *Environmental Quality—1976, the Seventh Annual Report of the Council on Environmental Quality* (Washington, D.C.: U.S. Government Printing Office, 1976), pp. 144–247.

7. "Impact of Government Regulations on General Motors." Paper provided through private correspondence, August 1977.

8. The McGraw-Hill Publications Company Economics Department, "5th Annual McGraw-Hill Survey Investment in Employee Safety and Health" (May 1977).

9. The equation (% price change) = $C_1 + C_2 Y_2 + C_3 Y_3 + C_4 Y_4 + C_5 REG$ was fitted by least squares to 35 observations on industry annual price change first for 1969–73 (where $Y_2 = 1970$, $Y_3 = 1971$, etc.) and then for 1973–77. The variable *REG* takes a value equal to one for observations for the regulated industries and zero otherwise. From these equations, $C_5 = 1.768$ and 1.617, respectively, with *t*

values of 1.56 and 1.0. For three *REG* variables, for mining (*REG* 1), automobiles (*REG* 2) and all other (*REG* 3), the values of C_3 1969–73 were 6.74, -2.63, and 1.66 with the first having a *t* value greater than two (so that the coefficient for automobile price increases was significantly different from zero).

10. For purposes of cross-industry comparison, given the small size of the metallic mining industry, the metallic and nonmetallic mining industries have been combined so that only seven industries are shown in the tables.

11. Pollution-abatement goals are in *Environmental Quality—1975, the Sixth Annual Report of the Council on Environmental Quality* (Washington, D.C.: U.S. Government Printing Office, 1975), pp. 569–71. Anne P. Carter, "Energy and Environmental Constraints," *The Bell Journal of Economics and Management Science* (Autumn 1974), pp. 578–92. Professor Carter's estimate from an input-output matrix was based not only on substantial diversion of capital for abatement but also on the use of labor and raw materials to operate and maintain the control equipment. It also assumes that currently proposed goals are going to be put into effect soon when, in fact, they have been modified or postponed a number of times. Thus the estimate probably overstates the growth reduction that is going to be realized.

12. Edward Denison, "Effects of Selected Changes in the Institutional and Human Environment upon Output per Unit of Input," *Survey of Current Business* (January 1978), pp. 24–44. The overall growth rate tends to be reduced because labor and capital which would have been used in measurable production are reallocated into activities whose output (worker safety, pollution abatement) is not a part of measured GNP. Thus output per unit of input is reduced by the value of services that productive factors would have provided if they had been used to produce final products. This value equals the opportunity cost of capital plus depreciation on diverted capital plus direct labor costs associated with meeting the standards. Denison's results indicate that output per unit of input was reduced as early as 1970, but especially since 1973. The cumulative effects of EPA and OSHA regulations reduced the level of GNP in 1975 1.4 percent below what it would have been had pre-1967 laws remained in effect. Denison's figures suggest that if the retardation of growth caused by EPA and OSHA regulations continues at the rate observed in 1975, the level of GNP could be as much as 5 percent lower by the mid-1980s.

13. Paul E. Sands, "How Effective is Safety Legislation?" *The Journal of Law and Economics* (April 1968), pp. 165–79.

14. Robert Stewart Smith, *The Occupational Safety and Health Act* (Washington, D.C.: American Enterprise Institute for Public Policy Research, 1976), pp. 87–88, Appendix A. Aldona DiPietro, "An Analysis of the OSHA Inspection Program in Manufacturing Industries, 1972–1973," draft Technical Analysis Paper, U.S. Department of Labor (August 1976). The analysis is based on regression equations estimated for 18 manufacturing industries where the firms have been classified as small, medium-sized, or large. With separate regression equations for each size group, workday accident incidence rates were explained by previous incidence rates and the occurrence of inspections. The coefficients for the inspection variable

were not significantly different from zero, but in a few cases they were both positive significant, indicating that the occurrence of OSHA inspections was accompanied by higher accident rates. DiPietro offered explanations for these perverse results: (1) incorrectly specified lag structures in the regression equations, (2) increased record-keeping in the companies raised the accident rate statistics but not accident rates, (3) higher accident rates encouraged more inspections. While the last is the most plausible, the main conclusion was that there was no evidence that OSHA activity reduced accident rates in these industries in the early 1970s.

15. John Mendeloff, "An Evaluation of the OSHA Program's Effect on Workplace Injury Rates: Evidence from California through 1974," report prepared for the United States Department of Labor (July 1976). The author used a regression model to explain the annual changes in the U.S. injury rate as a result of changes in new hire rates, lagged changes in new hire rates, changes in the percentage of male workers in the age group from 18–24, changes in the hourly average earnings of production workers and manufacturing, and a constant term. These factors explained 83 percent in the variation in the annual injury rate changes during these years and their net effect was to reduce the injury rate in the 1950s and increase it in the 1960s. Using the regression model to predict injury rate changes for the post-OSHA years, the author finds that the predicted (unregulated) accident rates were higher than actual rates but well within the prediction error of the model so that the two rates of change were not distinguishable. With respect to the California experience, similar regression analyses of specific injury types showed a decline after regulation but not significantly in most cases; also declines expected to be shown from OSHA's target-industry program occurred only in the lumber industry and only in one year but not in other target industries.

16. A. L. Nichols and Richard Zeckhauser, "Government Comes to the Workplace: An Assessment of OSHA," *The Public Interest* (Fall 1977), p. 55.

17. *Second Annual Report on the Administration of the National Traffic and Motor Vehicle Safety Act of 1966 for the Period January 1, 1968 Through December 31, 1968* (Washington, D.C.: U.S. Government Printing Office, 1969, Order No. 91-1:HDOC.110), p. 12. *1969 Report on Activities Under the National Traffic and Motor Vehicle Safety Act* (Washington, D.C.: U.S. Government Printing Office, 1970, Order No. TD8 12:969), pp. 9–10.

18. *Motor Vehicle Safety, A Report on Activities Under the National Traffic and Motor Vehicle Safety Act of 1966 and the Motor Vehicle Information and Cost Savings Act of 1972: January 1, 1975–December 31, 1975* (Washington, D.C.: U.S. Government Printing Office, 1976, Order No. DOT-HS 801 910), pp. 7, 10–11.

19. Sam Peltzman, *Regulation of Automobile Safety* (Washington, D.C.: American Enterprise Institute for Public Policy Research, 1975); H. G. Manne and R. L. Miller, eds., *Auto Safety Regulation: The Cure or the Problem?* (Glenridge, N.J.: Thomas Horton, 1976); and S. Peltzman, "The Effect of Safety Regulation," *The Journal of Political Economy* (July–August 1975), pp. 677–725.

20. Sam Peltzman, *Regulation of Automobile Safety*, p. 17.

21. Leon S. Robertson, "A Critical Analysis of Peltzman's 'The Effects of Au-

tomobile Safety Regulation,' " *Journal of Economic Issues* (September 1977), pp. 587–600. Dr. Robertson truncated the sample period, used data on youthful drivers (rather than on population), and deleted from the fatality statistics those observations related to trucks and motorcycles. His resulting equations showed that only speed and trend were significant in explaining accidents, and projections from the equation show car death rates that cumulate to 20 percent greater than actually occurred under regulation. But this suggests that there was a change in trend unrelated to regulation in 1965–67 as there had been in 1959–60. Moreover, there were important reductions in fatalities among pedestrians shown by Robertson's extrapolations to be attributable to regulation, when regulation in fact did little or nothing for their safety.

22. The Comptroller General of the United States, "Effectiveness, Benefits and Cost of Federal Safety Standards for Protection of Passenger Car Occupants," Report to the Committee on Commerce of United States Senate, CED-76-121, July 7, 1976. The main difference in approach between the Peltzman and GAO studies was that the latter was able to specify and differentiate pre- and post-regulation automobile model years and to use these differences to explain changes in mortality rates. But the comptroller's study failed to take account of demographic factors which were important in Peltzman's analysis for producing findings on agency effectiveness.

23. United States Council on Environmental Quality, *Annual Report* (Washington, D.C.: U.S. Governemnt Printing Office, 1977), p. 180.

24. Ibid. (1976), p. 272. For a number of years, severe dissolved oxygen (DO) depletion during the summer had been a critical problem in the Willamette River, to the point of causing the river to take on the characteristics of a running sewer. In the middle 1970s, summer DO levels increased to levels comparable to those in unpolluted waters, as a result of secondary treatment of all point source wastes and of stream-flow augmentation from expanded storage reservoirs. See U.S. Geographic Survey Circular 715, Part m, *Water Quality Assessment with Application to the Willamette River Basin, Oregon* (1977).

25. U.S. Environmental Protection Agency, "National Air Quality and Emissions Trend Report, 1976" (Research Triangle Park, North Carolina, 1976).

CHAPTER 4

1. The Federal Court of Appeals defined "dominance" to permit individual railroad rate setting only in markets where there were competing railroads. See *Commonwealth Edison Company* v. *ICC,* U.S. Court of Appeals, District of Columbia 76-2070.

2. Testimony of John Robson, Hearings on Aviation Regulatory Reform, Subcommittee on Aviation of the House Committee on Public Works, April 18, 1977.

3. Presidential Executive Orders 11821 (expired December 1977) and 12044 (issued March 27, 1978).

4. On February 27, 1976, OSHA released an inflation impact statement regarding emissions from coke ovens. The statement estimated that, for final demand, personal consumption expenditures would rise between .01 and .07 percent because of the new emissions standards. The study foresaw an increase in federal government defense spending of between .02 and .11 percent. Federal government spending for nondefense purposes was projected to rise at least .02 and at most .10 percent as a result of new standards (*Inflation Impact and Analysis of the Proposed Standard for Coke-Oven Emissions, 29 CFR 1910.1029,* [OSHA], p. 110). "These estimates have been obtained by calculating Laspeyres price indexes for each of the final demand sectors. This was done by taking a weighted average of price relations for the individual industrial sectors producing output for delivery to final demand. The Laspeyres index for personal consumption expenditures is comparable to the Consumer Price Index prepared by the U.S. Department of Labor, Bureau of Labor Statistics" (ibid., p. 109).

5. On December 7, 1976, the Council on Wage and Price Stability and the Office of Management and Budget issued "An Evaluation of the Inflation Impact Statement Program." The authors pointed out that "those who develop major regulations often pay little attention to economic analysis, at least initially. However, they are aware that at some point in the later development of the proposal economic analysis will be a 'necessary hurdle.' This awareness which has been sharpened by the IIS (Inflation Impact Statement) program, appears to have some effect on their efforts to identify alternatives and to assess costs" (p. iii). The evaluation, however, found that this effect varied from agency to agency. At EPA, "the IIS program, coupled with significant internal support, has succeeded in getting decision-makers to be more sensitive to economic analysis" (p. 51). The study found disagreement as to whether or not the IIS program had any measurable impact at OSHA. The authors do note that "the IIS program has resulted in OSHA's paying attention to both the cost and benefit sides as opposed to just considering the costs to firms or adverse effects to employment" (p. 68). The IIS program was considered successful at NHTSA. "The NHTSA staff members interviewed expressed the opinion that the IIS program has focused attention on the economic ramifications of proposed rules and regulations. This in turn is believed to have contributed to better agency decision-making" (p. 73). Though there were some problems with the IIS program, the evaluation concluded that the program was a success and should be continued: "The IIS program facilitates more rational decisions on proposals whose impact on the economy is substantial. It should be retained and strengthened" (p. 84).

6. *Industrial Union Department, AFL-CIO* v. *Hodgson,* 499 F.2d 467 (1974).

7. *American Iron and Steel Institute* v. *OSHA,* 577 F.2d 825 (1978), and *Society of Plastics, Inc.* v. *OSHA,* 509 F.2d 1301 (1975).

8. *American Petroleum Institute* v. *OSHA,* nos. 78-1253, 78-1257, 78-1486, 78-1676, 78-1677, 78-1707, 78-1745, slip op. at 80 (Fifth Cir., Oct. 5, 1978). Quotations used in the following discussion of this decision are at pp. 80, 90–91, and 93.

9. 569 F.2d 831 (Fifth Cir., 1978).

10. *Paccar, Inc.* v. *National Highway Traffic Safety Administration*, 573 F.2d 632 (1978); petition for writ of certiorari, U.S. Sup. Ct. (October Term, 1978), at p.

14. *Federal Register*, vol. 43, no. 203, pp. 48,648–49.

Appendix A

◇◇◇◇◇

Tabulation of
Regulatory Agencies and Activities

The following tables compile regulatory activities by agency or
state jurisdiction. This compilation is the same as given in the tables of the text, except that the activities are classified by agency
rather than agency being classified by activities. Also, more detail
is available here on financial, safety, and health regulation than
given in the text.

TABLE A.1 *Federal Regulatory Agencies Controlling Prices and Services*

Organization	Year established	Activities
Interstate Commerce Commission	1887	Controls prices, routes and service practices of surface transportation companies including railroads, trucks, bus lines, oil pipelines, and domestic watercarriers.
Federal Power Commission, now in the Federal Energy Regulation Commission of the Department of Energy	1930	Regulates wellhead gas prices and wholesale prices of natural gas and electricity sold for resale in interstate commerce.
Federal Communications Commission	1934	Sets prices for telephone and telegraph service, controls entry into telecommunications and broadcasting within the United States.
Federal Maritime Commission	1936	Controls fares and scheduling of transocean freight shipments.
Civil Aeronautics Board	1938	Regulates airline passenger fares, controls entry of airlines into city-to-city air routes, and provides subsidies to local service.

TABLE A.1 (Continued)

Postal Rate Commission	1970	Establishes classes of mail and rates for those classes; sets fees for other services.
Energy Regulatory Administration, (Department of Energy)	1974	Regulates wellhead crude-oil prices and refinery, wholesale, and retail prices of petroleum products; specifies allocation levels for wholesalers and retailers of crude oil, residual fuel oil, and most refined petroleum products produced in or imported into the United States during a period of energy emergency.
Copyright Royalty Tribunal	1976	Sets fees and charges on copyright materials.

SOURCE: *The Challenge of Regulatory Reform: A Report to the President from the Domestic Council Review Group on Regulatory Reform* (Washington, D.C.: U.S. Government Printing Office, 1977), pp. 50–51.

TABLE A.2 *Regulation by State Commissions*

Industry	Number of states regulating prices[a]	Number of states regulating entry
Electricity (private)	49	35
Electricity (public)	17	12
Electricity (cooperative)	29	23
Natural-gas retailing (private)	49	36
Natural-gas retailing (public)	17	11
Telephone	50	38
Airline service	21	25
Common-carrier trucks	47	45
Contract-carrier trucks	42	43
Railroad transportation	44	26

[a] Sales to ultimate consumers. (All totals include D.C.)

SOURCE: *1976 Annual Report on Utility and Carrier Regulation* (Washington, D.C.: National Association of Regulatory Utility Commissioners, 1977), pp. 392, 488, 594, 612, 615.

TABLE A.3 *Federal Agencies Concerned with Fraudulent Practices and the Security of Financial Institutions*

Organization	Year established	Regulatory function
Board of Governors of the Federal Reserve System	1913	Regulates commercial banks to reduce bank failure rates.
The Federal Trade Commission	1914	Administers laws concerning fraudulent and deceptive sales practices.
The Federal Home Loan Bank Board	1932	Supervises federally chartered savings and home financing institutions.
The Federal Deposit Insurance Corporation	1933	Supervises insured banks.
Securities and Exchange Commission	1934	Regulates investor information and securities exchange transactions.
Securities Investors Protection Commission	1970	Supervises and insures stock exchange transactions.
Farm Credit Administration	1971	Controls credit disbursed through the farm credit system.
Commodity Futures Trading Commission	1975	Sets terms and conditions for futures contracts and the exchanges trading such contracts.

SOURCE: *The Challenge of Regulatory Reform: A Report to the President from the Domestic Council Review Group on Regulatory Reform*, pp. 50–51.

APPENDIX B

Productivity Changes in the Regulated Industries [a]

Industry	1958–61	1961–65	1965–69	1969–73	1973–76
		(average annual rates of change in percent)			
Electricity	5.5	5.6	4.9	3.9	0.1
Gas	7.0	7.6	5.3	−0.1	−1.7
Telephone and telegraph	7.8	5.4	5.4	4.8	9.4
Railroad transportation	8.3	7.0	4.5	5.1	−0.8
Airline transportation	−0.9	10.7	3.0	2.4	2.0
Motor freight transportation	1.9	0.4	1.5	3.4	3.9
Unregulated service industries	4.8	3.6	2.9	1.6	−1.7

[a] Change in total output per man-hour.

SOURCE: U.S. Department of Labor, Bureau of Labor Statistics, Office of Economic Growth, unpublished data, November 1977.

APPENDIX C

Rates of Return on Book Value of Assets in the Regulated Industries [a]

Industry	1959-61	1962-65	1966-69	1970-73	1974-77
			(average annual rate in percent)		
Electricity	4.6	4.9	5.0	5.3	5.8
Gas transportation	4.8	4.9	4.7	5.2	5.7
Gas utilities	4.7	5.0	5.1	5.2	6.1
Telephone	5.1	5.2	5.2	5.4	5.8
Railroad transportation	5.4	3.3	3.3	3.4	4.2
Airline transportation	2.3	4.0	4.6	2.8	3.7
Motor freight transportation	3.4	5.5	5.8	5.9	6.1
Unregulated service industries	6.4	5.9	6.2	6.0	6.6

[a]Book value weighted average of retained earnings plus dividends plus interest payments divided by the book value of assets.

SOURCE: Computations from data in Standard and Poor's Corporation, *Compustat*, July 1977 revision.

BETA-Adjusted Rates of Return

BETA-adjusted returns are expected returns-to-investors that have been adjusted for the industry-specific risk premium (the BETA required by investors). A BETA coefficient is calculated for each industry over the period for which data exist (1958–77), according to the following formula:

$$\text{BETA}_i = \frac{\text{Covariance (Industry return, Market return)}}{\text{Variance (Market return)}}$$

$$= \sum_t (R_{it} - \overline{R}_i)(R_{mt} - \overline{R}_m) / \sum_t (R_{mt} - \overline{R}_m)^2$$

where R_{it} = Actual return to investors in industry i in year t

R_i = Mean return to investors in industry i over the period $(t = 1, 2, \ldots, T)$

R_{mt} = Actual return to investors in the market portfolio (weighted average of all firms) in year t

R_m = Mean return on the market portfolio

The average expected return to investors (R'_{it}) for industry i in year t is then derived according to the following formula:

$$R'_{it} = \overline{G}_t + (\overline{R}_{mt} - \overline{G}_t)\,\text{BETA}_i$$

where $\overline{G}_t$ is the rate of return on "riskless" assets (average annual rate of interest on 3-month Treasury bills) averaged over a given year-group

Values of $\overline{R}_{mt}$ (the average annual market return over a given year-group) are given in the tables as "Returns to Investors" for the Market. Values of G_t used in the analysis are as follows:

Year	Riskless rate	Year	Riskless rate
1958	1.839	1968	5.339
1959	3.405	1969	6.677
1960	2.928	1970	6.458
1961	2.378	1971	4.348
1962	2.778	1972	4.071
1963	3.157	1973	7.041
1964	3.549	1974	7.886
1965	3.954	1975	5.838
1966	4.881	1976	4.989
1967	4.321	1977	5.265

Index

price regulation in (early 1960s), 35–37, 39
price regulation in (late 1970s), 74–75
production changes in (table), 53
profit margins in, 48, 63
rates of return in, 49, 66, 67, 68, 74–75, 109, 110, 151
service quality in, 71, 73, 75
state rate cases for, 107–10
energy conservation policies, 98
Energy Department, U.S., 146, 147
Energy Independence Act (1975), 129n
energy industries, 19, 32, 33, 54, 59–60, 105, 126
Energy Policy and Conservation Act (1975), 137n
Energy Regulatory Administration, 147
entry regulation, 15, 17, 21, 31–33, 105, 123, 129n, 131n
industries subject to (table), 18
Environmental Protection Agency (EPA), 20, 21, 23, 83, 84, 87, 143n
benefits from, 94–104
cost effects of, 87–94, 126
current reform of, 115, 124
environmental regulation, 15, 17, 26, 29, 56, 81, 87–104, 105–6
benefits from, 94–104
cost of, 130n
organizations engaged in (table), 22–23
equipment standards, 28, 85–86, 87, 88, 95, 96–97, 102, 119–21, 122

Farm Credit Administration, 149
Federal Aviation Act (1958), 134n–35n
Federal Aviation Administration, 20, 22
Federal Communications Commission (FCC), 18, 20, 37, 50, 78, 79, 146
Federal Deposit Insurance Corporation, 149
Federal Energy Regulatory Commission, 18, 146

Federal Highway Administration, 22
Federal Home Loan Bank Board, 149
Federal Maritime Commission, 146
Federal Power Commission (FPC), 38, 52–59, 112, 114, 123, 146
Federal Railroad Administration, 22
Federal Register, 121
Federal Trade Commission (FTC), 131n, 149
Financial Institutions Act (1975), 129n
financial markets regulation, 16, 25
Food and Drug Administration (FDA), 20, 22
Ford, Gerald, 15, 16, 115, 129n

General Accounting Office (GAO), 99
Government Services Administration, 86
Great Society, 81, 83, 105
gross national product (GNP), 52, 70, 73, 89
health and safety regulation and, 92–94, 102, 106
in mid-1980s, 92–94
percent of, in regulated sector of economy, 21–24, 25, 105
growth rates, 29, 34, 50–52, 126

Health, Education and Welfare Department, U.S., 22
health and safety regulation, 15, 16, 17, 21–24, 25, 26, 81–104, 105–6, 139n
benefits of, 94–104
cost of, 130n
current reform of, 115–21, 122, 125
effects of, 28–29, 87–104
equipment specification in, 28, 85–86, 87, 88, 95, 96–97, 102, 119–21, 122
organizations engaged in (table), 22–23
proposals for reform in, 122–24
regulatory process in, 27–28, 82, 83–87
see also environmental regulation